Volume III

STORIES AND RECIPES
OF THE GREAT DEPRESSION
of the 1930's

Compiled by Rita Van Amber

Edited by
Janet Van Amber Paske
Home Economist

Seventh Printing   June, 2020

First Edition

ISBN 0-9619663-3-5

Table of Contents

About the Author

The author, Rita Van Amber, is an inspiring example of the strength and character which developed in the children of the Depression years. Born in rural Minnesota to hard-working German farmers, she was impressed as a young girl with the way her Mother held their family together during hard times. When there was little to prepare for meals, her Mother never let on to the difficulty of feeding her family, but kept a positive, encouraging attitude in the face of daily hardships. She considered it her responsibility to maintain the morale of her husband and children, and accomplished this through consistently serving delicious meals with the few ingredients available.

Rita attended grade school in nearby Millerville, Minnesota, at times boarding with her grandparents in town during the long winters. Upon completion of 8th grade, she was devastated to learn that she could not continue her education at that time due to family finances. Instead, she worked with several families, helping with meals and household chores.

People skills seemed to come naturally for her, and her desire for learning led her to earn a Student Nurse Certificate, which enabled her to provide in-home care for patients.

In 1939 she met an ambitious, energetic young man who captured her heart and her dreams. She admired George's positive personality and lively nature and determined she couldn't live without him. They married 3 months after they met, and celebrated their 50th Anniversary in 1989.

As a busy Mother of 4 children, also being fully employed, Rita realized the dream she had of completing her high school education. Many years of dedicated perseverance earned her the high school diploma she coveted.

Rita has also completed two years of college course work at UW Stout, but her work with Great Depression history through her three volumes of cookbooks has taken up most of her time in the recent past.

As a young child, Rita had developed an ambitious plan. She determined that she could start with something small and available, perhaps a pencil, trade it for something a bit more valuable, and continue on trading up until she had a house. This youthful fantasy actually became reality in her life when she and George opened and operated for 25 years a successful antique/junk shop. (Ideal Junque Shoppe)

Rita's persevering, positive attitude was definitely formed through her Mother's example during the Depression years, and has been an encouragement to the many lives she's touched since, but especially to her editor, who always poses one question when the going gets tough, "What would my Mother do in this situation?" In this way, the Great Depression has formed and affected this generation as well.

Lovingly and respectfully,
Her Editor and Daughter,
Janet Van Amber Paske

The author Rita Van Amber with her late husband George.

The author Rita with her daughter and editor, Janet.

IN GRATITUDE

Compiling Volume III of our "Stories and Recipes of the Great Depression" series has been a pleasure from beginning to end. The contacts we make with so many of you, from Menomonie, Wisconsin to Fairbanks, Alaska, from Dwight, Illinois, to Wolf Point, Montana, are all a treasure chest of mutual sharing of history remembered.

Your generosity overwhelms me. I am most grateful to each and every one of you who contributed to this work. To record for all time the experiences you lived during the most discouragingly hard times this country has thus far endured is a priceless contribution to the history of our young, capitalistic, free country. It is how we handled that painful universal problem at the home front that reflects the strong generation our parents and grandparents were. It is our heritage; a people who were willing to work hard, pull together, and make the best of the worst. It should never be forgotten.

Volume III is dedicated to all of you. Each visit by phone gave new inspiration. Each welcome letter so eagerly opened and read gave deeper insight of your unique, private circumstances in living that formidable decade in our history. You shared candidly from your souls and allowed your personal feelings to be documented.

Carl, thanks for never changing your values. Today we need to savor your guidance on fighting inflation. Roy, our Wisconsin crusader, thanks for having made this history one of your ministries. Buck S., we all will enjoy the benefit from your poignant memories of those challenging years. Beulah, we always knew the West was tough, you reinforced that. Isabelle, your children were your grave concern. Dorothy, you were always there for us in so many ways. Paul and Billy Fred, thanks for jogging my memory and adding to it. Marv, Clarence, Paula, Evelyn, Addie, Eddie and Edna, Ralph, Irene, and all the rest of you. You know who you are and you are all in Volume III and in my heart. My deepest gratitude to all of you and to those of you that I might not have found room for in this publication.

Each one of you has contributed to a history so long overlooked. We've read about government and business matters of the 1930's but have scant record from survivors; how men and women fought together to keep from sinking further into the muck of poverty; how children of all ages sensed it and understood. Family love and loyalty made all the difference.

A very special thanks also to Janet and Rich for your support and expertise in the mass of time consuming tasks you so willingly accepted. To Frank for being there wherever the need. To Micki for her creative cover design and John for his support. To Sam and Julie, Jeffie and Mary for your teamwork.

Thank you and God's blessings on all of you.

Rita Van Amber

Nothing captures the character and value of the women of the Great Depression as well as these words from
The Book of Proverbs.

"An excellent wife, who can find?
    For her worth is far above jewels.

The heart of her husband trusts in her,
    And he will have no lack of gain.

She does him good and not evil
    All the days of her life.

She looks for wool and flax,
    And works with her hands in delight.

She is like merchant ships;
    She brings her food from afar.

She rises also while it is still night,
    And gives food to her household,
    And portions to her maidens.

She considers a field and buys it;
    From her earnings she plants a vineyard.

She girds herself with strength,
    And makes her arms strong.

She senses that her gain is good;
    Her lamp does not go out at night.

She stretches out her hands to the distaff,
    And her hands grasp the spindle.

She extends her hand to the poor;
> And she stretches out her hands to the needy.

She is not afraid of the snow for her household,
> For all her household are clothed with scarlet.

She makes coverings for herself;
> Her clothing is fine linen and purple.

Her husband in known in the gates,
> When he sits among the elders of the land.

She makes linen garments and sells them,
> And supplies belts to the tradesmen.

Strength and dignity are her clothing,
> And she smiles at the future.

She opens her mouth in wisdom,
> And the teaching of kindness is on her tongue.

She looks well to the ways of her household,
> And does not eat the bread of idleness.

Her children rise up and bless her;
> Her husband also, and he praises her, saying:

"Many daughters have done nobly,
> But you excel them all."

Charm is deceitful and beauty is vain,
> But a woman who fears the Lord, she shall be
> praised.

Give her the product of her hands,
> And let her works praise her in the gates."

Chapter 1

If You Have
Walked the Walk
You Can
Talk the Talk

THIS WAS THE GREAT DEPRESSION

Eleven million Americans
    Out of work.
Franklin Roosevelt wins presidency
    In landslide.
Smile, smile, smile, the President said,
    And everyone tried to smile.
Immortal God Bless America,
    Sung by Kate Smith.
Orson Wells broadcast believed by many,
    Stirred up the nation.
Baseball came in strong, every city,
    Town and village had their team.
First College Football Cotton Bowl,
    1939 cost $6000.
Red Raiders vs St. Mary's College
    Started by Texas oil guru.
Mount Rushmore and Hoover Dam built by
    WPA workers earning $40 per month.
First Drive-in Theater opens in
    Camden, New Jersey.

THEY WALKED THE WALK

The Great Depression was a world wide phenomenon caused, in part, by maldistribution, as stated in Current History, 1932. There was no shortage of supplies, but there was a shortage of consumption. Due to the few rich saving and not consuming and the masses of the middle classes and poor not being able to buy, times soon reduced the middle class to poor.

Big business was blamed for hard times (McElvaine). Chase National Bank financier put millions into his wife's name and didn't even pay taxes on it. As banks closed, bankers and board members were suspected and in some cases tried for fraud and mishandling of funds.

The Disinherited Americans, as they were called (McElvaine), admired President Franklin Roosevelt to the point of sainthood. Letters would be addressed Saint Roosevelt. His Fireside Chats earned him the reputation of being the father and paternalistic guardian of the people. At his inauguration Roosevelt said, "the only thing we have to fear is fear itself". It is not possible today to believe what those few consoling words meant to comfort the impoverished people of that time. It was a forebodingly ominous feeling. Even the weather was radical.

In reviewing the early 1930's it's not hard to understand that people had become afraid of the future.

On August 19, 1929 a killing frost through the night destroyed crops and gardens. Government programs

4

implemented actually ran contrary to each other and became expensive failures. While farmers were able to weather both the drought and the depression in some areas, unfair land acquisitions by the government was more than they could bear. All too many lost everything and were driven off their land.

1930 and 1931 brought an extremely hot and dry summer with temperatures recorded in North Dakota at 114°. The fields and hay burned brown. It was the third year of the drought with heat related deaths totaling 1231. Patients brought into the hospital in Eau Claire, Wisconsin rarely lived. No refrigeration was available to cool the patients. At first, bushes and trees still produced fruit, but later entire orchards died out. It was also the beginning of the five day work week to spread the work around.

In 1932 wheat sold for 36¢ per bushel with field harvest at four bushels per acre. Fat beef sold for 2 1/2 ¢ a pound. Lean beef sold for 1¢ a pound. A 350 pound hog brought $2.00, which didn't even pay the shipping cost. Butterfat was 15¢ a pound and eggs dropped to 4¢ a dozen. Postage stamps went up from 2¢ to 3¢, and it was the year of the permanent wave.

In 1933 the Civil Conservation Corp (CCC) was implemented to take young men off the streets and give them meaningful paid work conserving natural resources. Teachers could not be married since only one in a family was allowed to have a job. Prohibition was amended Dec. 5. The page boy and curled bob was in. Mae West hit big time in "She Done Him Wrong".

The 1933 Civil Works Administration (CWA) put four million men to work on highways alone, plus massive sums for men to build dams to develop land.

The 1934 dust storms of the Great Plains lifted top soil off the earth and up in wind driven clouds of dust. Infants and elderly developed lung and breathing problems causing deaths. John Dillinger was gunned down as well as Pretty Boy Floyd and Bonnie and Clyde.

In 1936 cigarette consumption had climbed to 158 billion sold.

As we review this period in our history it isn't hard to see that there were benefits as well. Deprivation, worry and anxiety were always there, but the lessons learned from dealing with it and coping with the circumstances were a hidden bonus few, if any, counted on. In time our country grew strong and secure as a result. We ultimately won that bloody war, built our country up again, and demonstrated our democratic concern for other nations who needed assistance.

It was in 1934 that Franklin Delano Roosevelt called in all the gold. It had a value of $32.00 an ounce. Today it is worth in excess of $400 an ounce. You had no choice in 1934 but to relinquish it even though the government had no money to buy it. Money in the 30's was tied to gold.

Script paper vouchers were printed by the government to replace the gold. Several years later when the gold was accounted for the script was called in and real federally printed dollars were issued to replace the piece of paper. At that time money was not printed without a gold backing.

THE GREAT DEPRESSION THEY CALLED IT

It was more than that. It was also the great discouragement, the great despondency and the great despair at a national level. The fear and uncertainty of those times left it's mark on everyone. Even the affluent became worried wondering what the masses of hungry citizens might eventually do. Apprehension crept in like an ominous cloud and it stayed there. Never before had there been anything like it to give assurance that this too will pass. The rich and poor, young and old, grew up and older in a foreboding climate that was to change them forever.

The character of the men and women who lived it had to be admired for the strength and perseverance they demonstrated while living through it. Children grew up marked, not ever taking anything for granted again, living a lifetime believing it could happen again. And not trusting banks ever again after experiencing Black Friday in October of 1929. They had saved for a rainy day and when it came it was taken from them with no explanation of where it went. They always wondered who had it and where did it go.

The business world had ruled the country and now it had taken a disturbing setback. It too was struggling if not entirely bankrupt. Farms were being foreclosed on, sending people out on the road. If it wasn't you, it was someone you knew. And none of this was going away. It was becoming a lifestyle.

Angry letters began coming to Washington D.C., more and angrier all the time. These from respected members of society when they were "wiped out" and their families were going hungry.

Food riots began when crowds of men would break store windows and help themselves, first to the meat and flour and then the canned goods. The children had gone to bed hungry.

In Minneapolis a fire hose was used to dismantle the crowds and bring them under control after a merchant showed up with a revolver. His arm was broken in the shuffle.

In 1932 adolescents were riding the rails by the hundreds of thousands. They traveled in gangs or in groups for safety, comfort in loneliness and in illness. They congregated in hobo jungles where pots of food were being cooked. They brought whatever they could find, stolen garden produce, a chicken someone caught or just anything that could be cooked to make something edible. The suburbs became squalid jungles and a blight to the cities. Hoovervilles they called them. But no one feared these young men. They were not violent or distrustful and would work hard for any token payment such as a sandwich or anything to eat. They would work at anything for some food and then go on to look for more work. They rarely wrote home, stamps being 3¢ each. There was nothing to write about. But they all had a dream which was always there. It stayed with them wherever they went and propelled them on. Some day they'd strike it lucky and find work, anything at all, then they'd write home. And they'd put something in the envelope, as much as they possibly could.

At home the problems were big. No work, no crops, no rain, no help. Capitalism wasn't helping a nation in trouble, many were beginning to think. And then there was the election and the "Fireside Chats". Despair finally gave way to hope. New programs were mentioned and were rapidly implemented. Money in the form of grants was issued to each state to put family men to work. It wasn't much, but it was a God's send and it bought food. It lifted the fear men had been carrying too long.

A DECADE OF TRIALS

If society ever needed a reminder that we are meant to be our brother's keeper, the Great Depression was that reminder. The necessities it created brought people together like never before or since. It brought out the good in them as they shared with each other and gave to the hungry poor. People trusted and believed, speaking a universal language. They pooled resources and strength, struggling their way through a decade of extreme poverty.

The experience left those people with valuable character traits which served them well in later life. In fact those that lived it never lost it. They all are still connected to the Great Depression of the 1930's through never to be forgotten remembrances and stories by the people who lived it.

Each time we have a small recession, a doomsday "what if" begins to permeate the minds of Americans. When our security is threatened we become apprehensive. To our elders it means take no chances. Pay your debts, put some aside, be prepared. Having been hopelessly cheated of their birthright at one time, there is no guarantee it couldn't happen again. The fear, so far removed from the present, is always there. It's a trauma, having lived it makes it a permanent part of us.

We need to remember how it began and escalated and how our leaders dealt with the changes as they took place.

It had it's beginning in other countries and they weren't dealing well with it either. Signs began showing up in the large cities when unemployment began to rise. At first our administration refused to talk about it, saying it was a natural passing thing. It happens every now and then, they said, and will go away like it always does. Their thinking was that the government had no business to intervene and disrupt the lives of the sons of the pioneers. After all, they were rugged, strong, selfsufficient people and they'd take care of themselves. If push came to shove, there always was the Red Cross and the churches to help them out. But the Red Cross had no money coming in and the churches were also having money problems. People would help each other it was assumed. Hoover was adamant in his thinking the government had no responsibility in this matter.

WHERE DID THE MONEY GO?

Farms around Lake Elmo, Minnesota were ideal for raising strawberries. Rain in the 20's could generally be depended upon to keep the sandy soil moist for growing huge, sweet berries. There was a good market for the berries and it made an excellent side crop for the farmer as well as for his children. They earned 2¢ a quart for picking and it was the money that kept young Arndt Jensen picking every day for five weeks straight and sometimes longer. He valued his earnings and put it all into savings at the bank in his name.

The berries were picked to coincide with cream hauling to town so as not to make an extra trip. The berries were exchanged for groceries which were stored for winter use.

Arndt as a young boy was a good steady picker and a thrifty money saver. He was already looking ahead to his future. He wanted to be successful and knew that began with a bank account. He was proud of his efforts when he had saved $100. It was meant to stay there and grow until something very worthwhile came along when he was older.

In the late 20's there were rumblings of the money market beginning to be unstable. No one thought for a moment that it wouldn't settle down. By the fall of 1929 it became a worry and in October on a Friday the banks closed all across the nation, one after the other. You couldn't reach any bank by phone and there was no answer to knocks on the doors. The signs emphatically said "CLOSED". No explanations given. There was no one to talk to about it. It was a horrendous shock people had great difficulty dealing with. Many bank presidents were shot.

Arndt Jensen lost every penny he had saved picking 5000 quarts of berries. He never saw any part of his money again. It was a hard lesson to come to terms with and a severe blow to a young boy who had trust in our leaders.

Arndt Jensen
Menomonie, Wisconsin

Eva White remembers the time when her family had a dire need and money had to be withdrawn from the bank.

She recalls her mother walking to the village with the bank book. When she got there the door was locked and a sign starkly read, "CLOSED". Men were huddled on the street sharing their fears of what the future might yet bring now that their money was mysteriously taken from them.

This young mother came home without the much needed supplies and with the shockingly bad news. To worry and confuse the people further they were never told who had the money that was in the bank or where it went.

Eva White
Cornell, Wisconsin

NEED BROUGHT OUT THE BEST IN US

It was also a time in our ecologically uncertain environment when nature was not in harmony with man, when the earth which we not only had counted on but taken for granted, failed in producing the foods we needed to survive on. It didn't rain much anymore. We didn't think it could happen, especially not year after year.

Like never before in history, when the supply became seriously short, it was the women who were left holding the empty bag. Meals still had to be prepared for unbelievably large families, while babies came in spite of everything and the food supply dwindled. It was truly a time when it was up to the women to hold it all together at home. You hunkered down and made it work.

If you didn't know it before it became necessary to learn to make every spoonful count, and out of this necessity women became profoundly skilled at the art of thrifty homemaking. Never before or since has so much been expected of the cook unless it was the early pioneers.

In growing up the children learned from these mothers, believing this was a normal way of life since few had it

13

different. It was, as it turned out, the best education anyone could ever hope to acquire. No matter what else one did in life after that, knowing how to manage an efficient kitchen and home made everything else go better.

Children also learned that waste was strictly taboo. It was a crime against the family or anyone else for that matter since there was always someone out there needing it. Respecting ones resources was the rule. Whether it was a pay check or other material possessions, one was expected to handle it intelligently and with care. Thus it was with everything and particularly with the available supply of food.

And of course, vandalism was unheard of and would not have been tolerated. In a rare case of willful destruction, absolute restitution was expected and enforced, beginning with the parents in authority. It was a nice clean time to grow up. Wise parents instilled these values and virtues in their children as a way of life. It gave each member a place in the family unit with obligations to each other. Loyalty was the paramount virtue with parents setting the example. Sisters and brothers looked out for each other at home and away from home. It was a good comfortable feeling which lasted a lifetime. The large size of the families gave a substantial umbrella of security and experiences to draw from.

Fortunately, lessons of wisdom from that era live on. Man has always relied on knowledge acquired through experiences of previous generations. If we were to make all our own errors, life would not be long enough to make them all and it would be a lifetime of aimless frustrations filled with defeat and failure.

WPA ETHICS

They wanted to earn it, President Franklin Delano Roosevelt said on arranging money for the masses of poor. His WPA program was created "to provide the best kind of building of great public projects for the benefit of the public. Happiness lies not in the mere possession of money, it lies in the enjoyment of accomplishment". WPA would not just give a hand-out. It would give men back their self esteem and at the same time build communities to make them proud, build projects with lasting value. To this day their work stands as a testament to the fervent desire, not only to work, but to do their best. The WPA art project was an extension of this WPA program, giving to our country historical art work which would have been lost had it not been for the program. And the talented artists earned all of $40 a month, no more than the Works program recipients.

Projects varied widely for the men, selections being at the discretion of the county board. Improvements to the community were rated priority, such as tables and benches for the parks in cities, towns and villages; beautification of all kinds in every part of the country.

The men in the village of Elk Mound, Wisconsin, among other crafts, also made outhouses. Their work was superb craftsmanship. The outhouses were positioned in parks, church grounds, schools, wherever they were needed or could be used. In fact, before long they were hammering out more toilets than they found a need for. So they sold them, probably using the money for more supplies to do more work with.

All the while the county board was doing their best in coming up with plans for more work for the men. The WPA money grant was there, all they needed was to find a way to keep the men at work. To give more heads of families a chance at work they reduced the work days, giving shorter weeks, thereby giving more men work.

As time went by the problem became serious about what to do next. The directions from Washington D.C. stated, "to keep them busy, if nothing else build monuments to distinguish the community. Something they didn't have before; do something to keep them all happy," it said. "Smile, smile, smile." Roosevelt had said it would pull us out of this dilemma.

The Elk Mound board looked at the small village and at the terrain. The huge, steep peak to the west, no doubt, was spectacular. Why not build something on top of it to make it stand out further, for all travelers and locals to enjoy for all time. The men went to work with a vision in mind. First, a road had to be built up the steep pike. Then came the sandstone blocks razed from a crumbling livery stable, which had to be hauled up with teams of horses and wagons. On they worked until they had two stories of a look-out picnic shelter built. The third story observation tower gave a view of cities many miles away.

The edifice contained windows, had stoves for cooking inside, tables and benches for comfort and enjoyment, and a barbecue and an incinerator outside. All built large and very sturdily constructed. Steps came up on the outside, handrails were sunk into cement, all made to last forever.

It stands there today, weather beaten but still majestic. Reminding the world around it of a time when men begged for work, any kind of work for any kind of pay, while they worked their hearts out. (Photo on page 18.)

Marv Cartwright
Elk Mound, Wisconsin

A slogan of the 30's was:

> Good, Better, Best;
> May we never rest,
> Until our good is better,
> And our better is best.

D. S.
Stanley, Wisconsin

Picnic lookout at Elk Mound, Wisconsin, 1930's WPA Project

FAILED TOWNSEND ACT SETS STAGE

In 1933 when money was very scarce, Dr. France E. Townsend tried to promote an old age pension plan. The funds were to come from a 2% sales tax. Meetings were held all over the nation but the bill was continually defeated. Because so many people had been in favor of it, it was the forerunner of the Social Security act of 1935.

The Concise Columbia Encyclopedia

Submitted by
Virginia Winterfield
Sparta, Wisconsin

BANK CALAMITY CHANGED HISTORY

Social Security was initiated at a time when middle aged people had lost all they had worked and saved for. With no money, people lost their farms and homes causing millions of people to be out on the road and streets owning nothing.

Since the Depression lasted a decade, there was not time to recuperate from these losses adequately to provide for retirement. Our government saw a catastrophe about to happen to a generation of victims of that decade of financial disaster. In view of the growing numbers, knowing welfare would have to take care of them, the plan to build a fund for support through their own efforts was formed. It was

19

established for the working class since the Great Depression generation had many more productive years before they would need retirement income.

The payroll tax was implemented which would grow and accumulate for several decades before it was put to actual use. It was called Social Security. It favored the minimum wage earner in paying a larger percentage to them since they likely would have little or no savings at all.

Those were the original goals set out by congress in 1934 to replace handout welfare with a system to preserve the dignity and self esteem of people through their own earnings for future retirement benefits. The system worked well and the coffers began to bulge. However, subsequent leaders lost sight of the original goal. In place of investing it for growth they found ways to spend it, often to improve the program or to use for other purposes.

MY FAMILY RECOLLECTIONS

Chapter 2

The Tough
Got
Tougher

LIFE IN THE FOX SHACKS

Wisconsin people came to depend on the paper mills for their livelihood. It was work, even though the pay was not good for the long hours of hard work required of the men, it added up if it was steady. But gradually it became obvious that orders were slowing down considerably and the mills had to reduce their production. The heavy construction material manufactured at the mills and used for building wasn't in demand anymore. Likewise people couldn't afford other paper products any longer such as newspapers and magazines. Even schools used the same text books year after year. Children had to handle them carefully or the parents had to pay for them. Manufacturing companies using paper products had the same problem the mills had. Orders were not coming in, the demand wasn't there. It was a lonely frightening feeling not knowing what was going on.

Consequently paper mills had to cut hours to the bone, giving workers hardly enough to pay the monthly rent on the Fox Shacks. The shacks were constructed primarily of wall board and were built for employees and their families as living quarters. They did not get their name from the abundant population of wild life so numerous in the wooded river valley. It so happened the guru who owned and masterminded the plant operation was named Fox. The shacks were warm enough for the cold Wisconsin winters but they were always too small for a family. And families had a way of growing year after year. All the while women had an ongoing battle with bedbugs these paper shacks housed. It was a natural habitat for the bugs and it was next to impossible to keep them under control.

At least the men earned enough to pay for the housing and most realized how fortunate they were. It was a fact of the times that in other areas people were known to have been driven out of their homes with nowhere to go.

Most families had a cow and except for the years when it didn't rain, they always had large gardens with huge potato patches. A family could live off a garden all summer long and still have enough left to preserve for the cold months ahead. Food poisoning from preserving was rare even though all canning was done with the boiling water bath method. The real food culprits were warm pantries. The "summer complaint" was common which resulted from lack of refrigeration. The cellar floor or well pit kept foods cool but the pantry shelves were used for keeping many dishes for the next meal or day.

The cow produced milk which provided an enormous amount of food besides the large pitchers of milk on each table at meal time. There were puddings, soups, cheeses of all kinds and now and then some butter. Although cream was a cash crop and had to be skimmed off and sold at the grocery store for badly needed cash, some usually was allowed for the family as a treat. Lard often replaced butter for bread because there was plenty of it.

Chickens were literally sent from heaven to help people through the hard times. They too produced an income even when eggs sold for as little as 9¢ a dozen. You could buy quite a bit of sugar for bread baking for that amount. It added up and provided other necessities like coffee, hand soap, or a tin of Prince Albert for Dad. Not to mention the many meals one could make out of eggs. Sometimes entire dinners when meat was not available. At times when feed was hard to come by the chickens kept busy scratching for bugs and catching grass hoppers, oblivious to the rations shortage, and kept laying their fresh eggs. Then for all of this, when they were too old to lay eggs any longer, they ended up providing the best pot of chicken and dumplings in the world.

On a Sunday you might enjoy popovers made with eggs and a bit of whipped cream father allowed for this day. There was so much a mother could do to keep the family in good spirits if the outside world gave you a lemon. It sometimes was very hard but she expected it of herself, and she came through. The Great Depression war was won in her kitchen, there's no doubt about that.

PROUD APPEARANCES

It was a time when scruffy clothes were not popular. The proud people of the 30's would struggle hard to make it look good so as not to give away the depth of their poverty. Clothes were carefully brushed, washed, starched and ironed to make them look their best. Many were down to the last dress or pair of trousers.

Doris Fee made certain that her only dress was all-purpose. Her basic, dark colored sheath had sleeves and a slash at the neck. Being fashion conscious in a bankrupt world required creativity. Like everyone else she raided the family scrap bag for material to make collars and cuffs, dickies, jabots, belts, sashes, scarves, peplums, etc. Crocheted accessories were in, and competing with others for design and creation was a big part of the innovative style of the day. It brought out talents you didn't know you had.

Doris Fee
Hillsdale, New Jersey

SHOPPING A LA 1930's

We had mail order catalogs. In fact, the catalogs took care of 99% of our shopping needs. You didn't go to the county seat city any more than necessary. When you did go you packed a lunch, usually jelly sandwiches, because it was an all day trip. You had funds only for the barest necessities so shopping as such was a rare occurrence.

For this reason when the new spring and fall catalogs came out with new styles and items it was an occasion for excitement. There were several catalog companies, all of which sent a free catalog each season. Of course, if you didn't buy anything for a number of years, they took you off the list of free mailings. There were Sears & Roebuck Company, Montgomery Ward, and the M.W. Savage Co. They sold almost anything anyone would need, including the house with everything needed to build it, right down to the last door knob.Also the furnishings, the insurance policy to protect it all from any peril, and all clothing the family wore.

Goods were all made in the United States, and you could count on everything being well-made with no cause for returns. The manufacturer's reputation was at stake. No catalog had anything listed that was sold by another catalog. It made for great shopping at home. It could take several weeks to come up with a decision since you had to look through all the catalogs.

"Montgomery Ward catalog sales were almost too good to pass up. If somehow you could find the money, it bought quite a lot. For $2.00 a bundle you would get many pieces of fabric in all lengths and widths and colors. It was enough to sew shirts and dresses for the family for the entire year."

The late Helen Joos Cichy
Millerville, Minnesota

There also was the National Bellas Hess catalog with it's beautiful clothing. It wasn't often you could afford to order things from there, but you would examine the dresses and copy the styles using recycled old garments or material you could buy cheaper.

But the Spiegel May Stearns catalog, with it's unique merchandise, changed America's buying habits for all time. They pioneered in credit buying with payments to be made in monthly installments.

This system became overwhelmingly popular overnight because about this time many people had hit rock bottom. With the drought having devastated the farmers and no jobs of any kind to be found, living conditions became a serious worry. Things were wearing out with no money to replace them and no relief in sight. The poorer you became the more you were embarrassed by it since this had never been your way of life before. With the Spiegel catalog you now could replace the most necessary worn out items and pay a small monthly payment. In time it would be yours. Your attitude changed believing it was getting better now for sure.

But you didn't want anyone to see that the Spiegel catalog was being used in your house. It meant you were charging goods. This too was embarrassing, so you kept the catalog out of sight.

You could buy as long as your credit was good. Missing a payment only once was bad for your rating. If your name ever would have been listed with a collection agency you were black balled for life. It would be cash and carry forever after so you made sure it would never happen. Before long Sears and Montgomery Ward were joining the plan and credit buying became a way of life.

$6.00 BOUGHT EVERYTHING

In most cases buying new clothes was the least of our worries. We wore what we had. Business for mail order companies had dropped so drastically that companies were coming up with new gimmicks to generate sales and to lure people into buying.

Buck Stahlbusch saved his money, and when the catalog came out offering an entire outfit of clothes from head to toe... hat, shoes, belt and socks for only $6.00 plus 15¢ postage, he was ready to order.

Measurements had to be exact from the head size down, including the neck, waist, arm length, trouser inseam, belt size, shoes and hose. When the package arrived every item fit perfectly.

Buck wore his handsome new outfit only once before he was called into service for his country. Several years later when he came back he expected to find his new clothes waiting for him in the closet where he had left them, but everything was gone. Others in his family had grown into the new clothes and had made good use of them while he was wearing his military uniform. (Photo on page 32.)

Buck Stahlbusch
Elk Mound, Wisconsin

———————————

Buck Stahlbusch in his $6.00 mail order outfit.

YOUR HOUSE KEY WAS STORED AWAY

No one ever locked their doors. What for? How would the ice man get in? The square card in the window with a number on each side told him how much ice was wanted and everyone else that drove or walked by knew the door was open.

If you ordered groceries and had to leave, money was layed out in the appropriate place. The delivery boy made the change and put perishables in the ice box. If you had fresh cookies you had several on a plate for him.

We enjoyed this freedom into the 40's and even 50's, always leaving for vacations for weeks at a time when at least the back door was left open. It was the Great Society concept of the 60's that changed all that. Federal programs were mandated to assure that "all men were created equal" in our country. It had the resultant effect of dividing the classes and creating new subcultures previously unknown in America.

YOU TOOK THE BAD WITH THE GOOD

"Few farms in the rural areas of Minnesota had electricity in the early 30's and ours was one of the no-haves," remembers P.A. Cichy, now of Minneapolis, Minnesota. "We had a radio, although the batteries were low or dead most of the time. As a result we went to the neighbors to hear the Joe Louis fights.

We all sat around the radio looking at the speaker, visualizing the action of the fights. We seemed to get a better picture of the action through our imagination than we do today with the finest TV's.

After the fights someone would pop a large bread rising pan heaping full of popcorn. The corn was popped in the big old iron all purpose skillet every household had. Pure home rendered lard was used and no salt was added. It was dumped on the oil cloth covered farm table with everyone sitting around enjoying the treat and the lively banter that ensued. We enjoyed these evenings immensely."

"One morning in July my parents awoke at 2:00 AM to a very bright light outside all over the yard. Perhaps there was a combustion sound that might have awakened them, and seeing the yard lit up like high noon was alarming. The barn was burning. The hay mow of the big red cattle barn was a huge inferno. We were called downstairs and instructed to run to the neighbors, one in each direction a mile away, to call the fire department.

There were no private numbers on those old phones. Codes were used, and when a number was called, and especially when it was the fire department number, and at 2:00 AM, everyone jumped out of bed to hear where it was. Sometimes it was a house with kids upstairs; this was a barn with cattle in the pasture. But the people came. Part out of curiosity and part to help, which they tried to do.Cars kept coming until it looked like a big summer auction, parking far out on the road-side to stay away from the sky full of flying timber sparks. The fire department concentrated on saving the house and preventing the sparks from igniting it. There was nothing they could do for the barn, it burned to the ground. The cows came home on their own that morning, looked around, and some even tried to go to the exit of the barn door to get in for milking.

Our barn was insured for $1500 but the insurance company said because of the years of depreciation they could only pay half of that. The barn had been in excellent condition.

The entire community came to help get the barn replaced. They each worked a day free and for $1 an hour after that. They worked hard and fast and had the barn up in no time. The foreman however, was paid more money. He got $1.35 an hour straight through.

My parents gave an appreciation dance in our huge kitchen. Two local people came to play and Mother had lots of lunch and coffee. It was prohibition but there were bootleggers outside."

P. A. Cichy

THE "LONE WOLF" TRADER

There is a "Lone Wolf" picture in our family which we all admire more than if it had been a Rembrandt or Gough masterpiece.

In the 1930's nothing new ever came our way for so many years we had all but forgotten there were beautiful things out there, albeit far out of our reach. We never went to town just to look around or to window shop. It was frivolous to expect anything.

But one day we were surprised when an old beat up Ford truck with high side boards on it's box came clattering down our drive way and a tattered old man got out. He explained that he was buying junk copper and brass from cast off old items one might have lying around. When asked what it might be worth to him, he said he bought by the pound and since he had no cash either, he gave a beautiful picture of her choice to the lady of the house. My father was delighted with the prospect of arranging a gift for my Mother so easily. Nothing had come easy for so long and certainly nothing to beautify the home with.

My father was impressed with the man's efforts in making a living practically by begging people for their junk. He took him around the farm, behind the machine sheds and barns, out in the family dump where he found a considerable amount of good solid brass and copper pieces of all kinds. At one time these metals were used extensively and exclusively for certain parts of machinery, buggies and surreys, so the dumps and trash piles, which every farm had, were full of them.

The man took his time searching and declined a cup of coffee my Mother offered. When he was satisfied that he had looked the farm over sufficiently and his truck was nicely filled, he invited my Mother to come out and choose the picture she liked best for her wall.

Mother studied the pictures carefully and liked them all so well she had difficulty selecting, but finally chose the "Lone Wolf" picture she saw my father admiring.

We all loved it and considered it a gift from the poor, kind, old man. The picture is still in our family possession and is cherished for the memories it holds. Each day it becomes more valuable as an antique but it is stored with our family memoirs.

I was a child at the time and I remember being impressed by the old gentleman. He was working at making a living with discarded old junk and wasn't too proud to dig in the dirt for his livelihood. This memory stayed with me.

Later we heard the market for brass and copper was going up and this was an ominous sign of impending war in the not too distant future.

Decades later, when time allowed, I found myself in the business of buying old stuff and reselling it, just like the tattered man had years ago. It was a good fulfilling feeling. A yearning had come full circle. I called our business "The Ideal Junque Shoppe", and operated it for many years out of a recycled old school building called the Ideal School.

R. V.
Menomonie, Wisconsin

———————————

SHARING THE COAL

"We often talk about how neighborly and helpful people were during the Depression, how they pulled together", writes Beulah Tufton of Wolf Point, Montana. "And this attitude hung on even after times got better. This was never demonstrated better than when a great blizzard hit Plentywood, Montana. Shortly after the storm hit, which was in late March, the local dray man, Elmer Gooder, pulled into town with a truckload of coal. It was destined for some place or other but he wasn't foolish enough to try to keep going. He tied up at the Lincoln Lumber Co. where my dad worked then. The storm continued to rage and the temperatures kept going down. Elmer began to wonder if people had enough coal to last them through the storm since it was late spring and lots of people let their coal supply dwindle in anticipation of spring and summer. There were too many places to use the money to allow buying six months ahead.

Elmer called on volunteers to sack his coal and haul it on foot and sleds from house to house where they were running out, pulling the sleds through blinding snow and cold, giving it to them free.

On the third day they ranged further out and came upon a little house occupied by an elderly retired school teacher. There was no response to their knock on the door, so they walked right in. No doors were ever locked. They found her sitting in front of her kitchen range which had the barest little fire in it, wrapped in blankets with her feet in the oven.

She started to cry when the two snow covered men burst

into her kitchen. She was almost out of coal when the storm hit and had burned about everything in the house that would burn. She was prepared to die. There was nothing else to burn. The two men got the stove going, made her some coffee and warmed up the soup she had on hand. They also left her an extra sack of coal before they were on their way to check on others."

B. Tufton
Wolf Point, Montana

EARTHQUAKES WERE MINOR INCONVENIENCE

"The year was 1935 or 36 when we had a minor earthquake in our capital city of Helena, Montana. My dad worked for that marvelous "old man Fretheim" hauling produce from the Spokane area. Dad and Mr. Fretheim got to Helena in the evening of the earthquake and they were going to spend the night there. Dad refused to check into the hotel, so he slept in the truck. Mr. F., who was never afraid of anything, checked into this little hotel that had the whole front wall missing, leaving those rooms open to view. Dad said he didn't get much sleep. Every little after shock woke him up and scared him to death. Mr. F. on the other hand had a really good night's sleep. Today that hotel would be condemned because of the damage, but yesterday was a totally different time and if things were usable, they were used. Except for the missing front wall, the hotel was in good shape. Of course, everything built then was sturdier than it is now.

Beulah Tufton
Wolf Point, Montana

Living in a large city in the 30's had it's advantages. You didn't have to be very old to earn money working and if you were a hustler you could sell newspapers. Of course you handed all your earnings over to a parent who would always give you a nickel or so for pocket money. A young lad in the city loved to have a coin in his pocket and it provided a first class lesson in learning how to handle funds.

Even small earnings went quite a long way in San Francisco where a boy could swim all day for a nickel. For free you could surf fish from the Embarcadero all the way to Fly Shacker's Pool. And there was a community hall where kids could learn to do crafts in the evenings. There was always a choice of things to do in the city. But you had to work for your money. Children learned that lesson when very young.

F. R.
Cornell, Wisconsin

MY FAMILY RECOLLECTIONS

Chapter 3

Somehow
Life Went On

THEY DIDN'T GIVE UP

Every effort was made to keep on doing business as usual. In spite of the severe shortages, many places kept their doors open by devising a way to help their customers. There was nothing else out there for them, so they struggled on, all the while praying for better times.

Creameries would furnish feed for the livestock, butter, cheese and other dire needs as a draw against the cream checks. Often times the customer owed the creamery at the end of the month, but they worked it out on the next check.

The meat market kept afloat by going to farms to kill and dress out their livestock and take it back to the market to cut up and to use for store sales. The farmer could draw beef against the animal that was picked up.The butcher took his income out of a percentage of the meat.

COMPETITION WAS KEEN

It took initiative and stamina and an urgent yearning to get out from under to keep from failing in any new business. Most of the old had folded or were barely hanging on. To survive in the economy of the 1930's you had to have something needed by many and you had to know something about marketing. But the public was hard to change. Money was too hard to come by for anyone to venture into the unknown and try anything new. Since you couldn't gamble with a dollar you stayed with the old and tried and true. It was safer that way.

In starting a new business you soon learned there were obstacles you hadn't known anything about. For starters, there was the everlasting shortage of cash and the banks didn't help much. Since Black Friday they were unusually cautious of failed loans and no one blamed them. People weren't buying much of anything and definitely not something they knew little about. Too many were trying to sell something and few bought. You had to have something good and you had to have the expertise to let customers know about it.

It took witty new ideas, an innovative enterprising approach and a number of failures to learn from for a chance at success. Few succeeded, but the Odell family of Minneapolis, Minnesota knew they had a product better than any thus far. Together they had the persistence to surmount the setbacks and failures to keep going on. They combined their ideas and efforts and through trial and error and very hard work they succeeded in eventually making an enormously successful business out of shaving soap. They called their company the Burma-Vita Co. and their product Burma Shave.

The usual method of shaving had been the mug with it's

round fitted soap and a brush. The company had to find a way to not only perfect a lather cream that did a better job of softening stiff whiskers in order to get a closer shave but also to convince a cautious public to try it. There were a lot of gimmicks being used that were a waste of money. Advertising was difficult because people weren't buying a lot of newspapers or magazines and radio advertising was in its infancy and not yet proven to be worthwhile.

A young son of the family, an entrepreneur like his father, came up with the idea of trying a series of highway signs to make their product known. The group discussed it and then decided on how to do it best. They came up with using a clever catchy verse, printed in bright colors on signs a number of feet apart so they could be easily read while driving the speed of cars of that day. The first trial series did bring in business so they expanded. With each new series of signs in new areas the business grew noticeably. They were on their way. To get new fresh verses they held a contest giving $100 for each verse sent in that was selected to use. Hundreds of thousands came in all vying for the big money. So many, in fact, that an office had to be established and people employed to make wise selections for the signs springing up all over the nation. Fearing the highway department might frown on the distraction to the drivers, they quickly took advantage of the situation and made a priority of putting up signs that encouraged good driving habits. The highway department loved it because it also carried their safety message.

REMEMBER THIS
    IF YOU'D BE SPARED

TRAINS DON'T WHISTLE
    BECAUSE THEY'RE SCARED.

                        BURMA SHAVE

THEY MISSED THE TURN
    CAR WAS WHIZZ'N

FAULT WAS HER'N
    FUNERAL HIS'N.

                        BURMA SHAVE

IS HE LONELY
    OR JUST BLIND

THIS GUY WHO DRIVES
    SO CLOSE BEHIND.

                        BURMA SHAVE

HE LIT A MATCH
     TO CHECK GAS TANK

THAT'S WHY THEY CALL HIM
     SKINLESS FRANK.

                      BURMA SHAVE

DON'T TAKE A CURVE
     AT 60 PER

WE HATE TO LOSE
     A CUSTOMER.

                      BURMA SHAVE

The public loved the light hearted flirty verses and the masculine shaving signs made Dad and big brother feel good about themselves. It created a nice feeling and it seemed to lighten the load. It was something to smile about. President Roosevelt had said, "Smile, smile, smile, it'll get better". The Burma Shave people gave this country something to smile about.

Burma Shave was on it's way when the war broke out and

the government issued a can in every military man's first aid kit. Sprayed on a wound, it eased the pain and burn of phosphorous from grenades and bombs for the men in heavy fighting.

BETTER THAN NOTHING THEY SAID

Work didn't get you much if you were a farmer in the 1930's. Chickens were easiest to raise and they did provide a little cash, even though it was sorry little at 7¢ a dozen for eggs at one time. Cleaning out the coops wasn't all that bad and when the faithful birds had their life's work in, as a grand finale, you got a terrific dinner from your feathered friend.

And every farmer had pigs. There was a time earlier when you could count on a nice check every fall to pay off a part of your farm or whatever. They were easy enough to raise, only needing their feed regularly. The hogs were happy with whatever living arrangement was provided, but they brought nothing on the market now. So you butchered all you could use, canning, brining, smoking and using the rest fresh, to provide meals year around. The large amount of lard rendered as part of the butchering was used heavily in all baking and frying. The pigs supplied meals but brought in no badly needed cash.

But the herd of cows which were meant to provide you with your livelihood was a frustrating commitment. You had a bear by the tail and you had to hang on. To feed the animals it took cutting, hauling and stacking hay and seeing they were fed daily. You cleaned the barn out every 24 hours and hauled it out to the fields. You already had many hours of work invested and you hadn't started milking yet which was done by hand as well as the milk separating. Several times a week your cream was picked up or you hauled it to the creamery yourself. For all of this you got a small check, around $25 or $30 a month if you were milking ten cows. The cream check had to buy everything the house, car and family or farm needed to make it another 30 days. Butter fat was down to 11¢ a pound.

When you analyzed your long hours of work, often before the break of day till late at night, you made pennies an hour. And it took the entire family to do it. It was a discouraging work, but you had your home, and you had food. The reports you heard of millions elsewhere out of work, with no jobs to be had and no home, kept you right on working for the security of your farm for as long as you could hang on.

FARMING NO PIECE OF CAKE IN COLFAX, WISCONSIN IN '34

With pastures burned up from lack of rain and thousands of dairy cows facing starvation, the government realized it had to do something for the farmers in Wisconsin.

They agreed to pay the shipping costs of the lean cows to ship them a few hundred miles up north to the lakes and woods area where the drought had not been quite so severe and the lake banks provided something green for the cows to graze on. The woods gave the animals shade to escape the burning summer sun, which some days drove temperatures all the way up to 104°.

While milking cows were dried up so the animals could gain some weight, one cow was saved for milking. The herdsman had to eat. To round out his diet he found berries and had them with cream and shot rabbits and either fried them or stewed them in a pot. Now and then he fished and fried the rewards over the camp fire. It was a long and lonely summer for him.

A herdsman soon learned he needed a good horse. Out west anyone could round up wild range horses, break them so they could be handled, and make good riding horses out of them. Albeit wild, but very useful. The herdsman and his horse quickly became a team weathering the blistering summer together.

The grazing area was around the lakes, the brush and the woods, with the cows running free. Ear tags were used to identify cows, and to locate them the herdsman listened for the bells. A few of the animals wore cow bells, fastened to leather straps around their necks.

When summer came to an end, it was the herdsman's responsibility to get the herd home. Either he paid $2.00 a head to have them shipped home by rail or he walked them home himself.

Back home in Colfax the summer of '34 had been unbearably hot with temperatures reaching 108° at times. Everybody did their work just the same and at days end would grab a bar of soap and a towel, strip down to nothing and plunge into the clear cool water of Elk Creek near Colfax.

You couldn't sleep in the overheated house but tried to be first to get the car cushions to sleep on for the night. There were no mosquitoes but the fire flies proliferated and multiplied with hundreds of thousands blinking their bright lights all night long, telling the world it was good to be alive.

H. Stahlbusch
Colfax, Wisconsin

RECYCLING WAS PART OF MANAGEMENT

On the farm, recycling was more than a way of life. It made survival possible and was good management. It grew with your operations.

You even recycled water four or five times before it ended up in the horse drinking tank. If you had piped your water it started icy cold in the house straight from the well, then on to the cream cooling area, to the cattle drinking cups in the barn and finally to the stock tank for the horses, all the same water.

You could go wild with corn stalks. Chopped up they made excellent night feed for the cattle. Rough stalks left over in the morning were tossed under the cow as bedding. The next morning it was swept into the manure gutter as an absorbent. You treated your livestock well and they returned the favor.

Pigs too got their tender loving care. Charcoal was salvaged from the ashes of the wood burning stove after it had heated the house. The charcoal was fed to the pigs to aid digestion. The wood ashes were scattered on the garden and around berry bushes to give nutrients for healthy growth.

And you raised your own seed from year to year from your best fields and your choicest garden plants. Flower seeds too were gingerly saved and labeled for spring use. You passed seeds on to others, especially if you had a special tomato or spinach or extra beautiful blooms on flowers. You always saved more than you needed to share with others.

Corn seed, however, was tricky and had to have special attention. It had to come from your most productive yield. Hand selected ears were hung to dry from the ceiling of the upstairs or attic so mice wouldn't get them. They were woven onto a string so the cobs didn't touch and were left there until spring. When the corn was taken down for seeding in spring you hand shelled it using only the middle kernels of the cob. Mechanical shelling damaged the germination area. The ends usually were not uniform and you wouldn't want to plant that grade. The remainder of the cobs with corn still left on them were fed to the horses. They loved this treat and ate cobs and all.

Corn had to be tested for germination before planting. You would count out 25 kernels and place them on a wet newspaper. This would be rolled up and placed in a warm place near the heater. Ten days later you opened the paper and counted the kernels that showed growth. This gave you the germination percentage and you planted accordingly.

But of course, your work with corn hadn't begun yet. It was planted using a cable to make straight rows across the field both ways and diagonally. The crop was a beauty to observe as it grew by day and night, like a work of art in the vast field.

Cultivating was done regularly throughout the growing season. You cultivated twice with the two row cultivator, once with the sulky cultivator and yet another time with the walking cultivator with face masks on the horses so they wouldn't sway from the path nibbling on the rich green leaves.

It was long, hot, dusty work but you did your very best to get a crop out of the parched soil.

Harold Stahlbusch
Colfax, Wisconsin

FALL OF 1929

Somehow the word got out that the banks were soon to close their doors and all savings would be gone. An Elk Mound mail man did his customers a favor by tipping them off so they could hurry to the village to get their money out before this happened.

His first stop when he got back was to go to the bank, but it was too late. The sign on the door said "CLOSED", with no notice when it might open again. His life savings and nest egg were gone, all $150. It was a woeful feeling not knowing what the future would bring.

Harold Stahlbusch
Elk Mound, Wisconsin

TRADING SOLVED FINANCIAL PROBLEMS

With cash flow at a virtual stand-still, trading often was the only way to do business. Even banks negotiated deals unheard of before in an effort to keep business alive and their doors from closing again.

George Van Amber's 1931 Pontiac Sport Coupe

Young George Van Amber, of Alexandria, Minnesota, couldn't meet his car payments after being injured at work. It was a 1931 cherry red Pontiac Sport Coupe, heavy with chrome and fenders. (Photo on page 57.) The bank had to repossess it. But he had some equity in it and couldn't afford to lose that. It was all he had.

The bank officials conferred and came up with a deal. George would take possession of a cow which had been taken from a farmer to make good an overdue payment on a loan the farmer had defaulted on.

George was staying with relatives while out of work and could hardly lead a cow home for them to supply feed for. They were already feeding him all winter.

After explaining his dilemma to the bankers, they conferred again and found a sale for the cow for George through a loan another farmer was getting to buy livestock. The deal was that the farmer would get a smaller loan and take the cow. George got a part of his equity back and everyone seemed to be satisfied.

TRADING REPLACED CURRENCY

We had a lot of pigs and prices were so low we couldn't pay the shipper out of the proceeds. We also couldn't feed them because the corn crop had burned up. We heard of a farmer who needed pigs for butchering for his large family. My father went over to see him and came home with a horse we badly needed in exchange for our pigs. We thought Dad made a terrific deal. No doubt the farmer with all the pigs felt very fortunate since they could eat well all winter long.

Paul Cichy
Brooklyn Center, Minnesota

THE BARTER EXCHANGE

"I was trying to save up enough money to buy a washing machine when I got married so I wouldn't have to use the wash board. Then the banks closed and the Great Depression began. I was working at the hospital at the time and got most of my meals plus $25 a month. Then I got married and $10 went for rent for three rooms and a toilet, $5 went for furniture paid on the installment plan and $10 was left for us to eat. Milk was 10 cents a quart from the creamery. My new husband Clarence went every day to try to get work and came home with no results. He was so depressed, I felt sorry for him.

There was a Barter Exchange. It was a kind of store where they carried unperishable goods such as rice, beans, etc. and some household articles. Clarence washed windows, storms, anything one needs done around a house and they gave him a slip of paper giving the hours he had worked at that job which he could exchange for items we needed.

No one had any money. He finally got a job at a sash and door plant paying 15¢ an hour. But the plant burned down and he was out of work again until it was rebuilt. We had to get out of our rented place because the owners needed it themselves.

My father helped us buy a lot and we put up a 9 x 9 tent. By that time we had a year old daughter and we lived in that tent 3 1/2 months while Clarence tore down an old building and built a two room house. We had a day bed that would open up and a trunk to put our clothes in. Since Clarence worked nights, Ginger and I slept in the day bed. When Clarence needed a bed too, I made a bed on the trunk.

It was a hot summer and every other day it rained. We had to sit in the car so Clarence could get some sleep in the tent."

Irene Treu
Wausau, Wisconsin

CITY FATHERS CAME UP WITH SOLUTIONS

Winters of the 1930's were known to be very severe and people had a constant worry about being able to have money available for heating fuel.

Suicides became a common way to deal with insurmountable problems. Men felt they were failures when there wasn't enough food in the house to go around or fuel to keep the family warm. Some even lost their farms and had no home to heat.

Eau Claire, Wisconsin came up with a solution to help people. The city purchased the wood off a large acreage of woods owned by a farmer not far from the city. The area was along highway 29 and county T. The wood was divided into lots and allocated to the needy who could go there with their hand saws and cut what they needed.

Immediately the problem to haul the wood home came up and the men solved that problem by salvaging old broken down cars, using the wheels and axles to build trailers. Soon Ford Motor Company heard of this and before long they were manufacturing conversion kits. They sold inexpensively and made a very good sturdy trailer for any use.

A wood cutter could be contracted to cut the wood up into pieces but there seldom was money to pay him. If you had a pig you'd offer it for payment. Of course he wanted it butchered and dressed out which was done right then and there and hung to cool overnight for the man to pick up the next day. If he ended up with too many dressed out pigs he bartered with the grocer for groceries or other items he needed such as gas and oil for his equipment.

Harold Stahlbusch
Tainter Lake, Wisconsin

WE DID WITHOUT

Martha Mikkelson of Wausau, Wisconsin, recalls, "It was in the early 30's, one of those summers when we were having a real drought. Day after day went by and it didn't rain. No crop grew, not even the grass. Everything was dry and brown. As we walked across the fields, the grasshoppers were so thick they would get into our hair and down our necks. There was no grass for the cows to eat, and we had no feed for them. They got thin and gave very little milk. Dad cut down trees in the pasture so they could eat the leaves, but this was only a temporary solution.

The drought never let up. Some friends of ours at Wayside, Wisconsin, near Green Bay, heard of our plight and offered to take our cows and keep them and feed them through the winter. Since this was a way out for us we took them up on the offer, hoping for a better season the next spring and summer. They came with a big truck and hauled away our cows, and with it our livelihood. Eight cows was the most we could keep in our barn. One was sold for $8 so we'd have some cash. Their pay would be to keep the calves in the spring. We made it through the winter and in spring they brought the cows back and we resumed farming. The following spring and summer we finally had some rain.

This was a hard winter for us with no income except for the chickens. Eggs were saved and taken to the grocery for necessary groceries. We learned to do without many things but the hardest job fell on Mother, who had to use her ingenuity to feed us through that winter. As a result we often had strange things to eat that we did not like.

One such recipe she brought home from the neighbors, who had fourteen children to feed. It was a flour soup, made with flour and water, seasoned with salt and pepper and some butter. This, together with good home made bread and butter made a meal for us. I don't remember that she made this very often as it just didn't taste good. As a rule, we couldn't be picky about our food but ate what was put on the table.

During one of these Depression years there was a milk strike. We couldn't sell any milk, but just had to dump it. During this time we all drank a lot of milk. In fact, Dad drank so much that he got a gall bladder attack and had to go to the hospital for surgery. We blamed the milk but it probably wasn't that at all.

It was hard to dump the milk, since the money was our livelihood. We did skim the cream from the top and used that to make butter by shaking a 2 quart jar. We took turns for this. If we didn't have any money at least we had plenty of milk and butter. That probably contributed to the fact that three of my sisters have had heart surgery and I have had angioplasty.

Another summer it rained all the time and our potatoes rotted in the ground, but the rutabagas did exceptionally well. That winter we ate rutabagas day in and day out. We had so many we even fed them to the cows.

Growing up in the Depression we learned to do without and we are probably better off now having had these experiences."

Martha Mikkelson
Wausau, Wisconsin

THE PARSON WAS ALWAYS THERE FOR THEM

"We lived in Minnesota, in a rural community of Bohemian farmers. When the bottom fell out of the grain market and the banks foreclosed on those who couldn't make payments, the despair overcame many of those rugged souls. They jumped from the barn roof or hanged themselves from the high beams. At that time the Catholic Church did not bury suicides and my father, a protestant minister was often called to serve these families. At one time, during the darkest hours of the Depression, he had fourteen of these funerals in two weeks.

Tramps were an ever present fact of life at our house. They figured a parsonage couldn't turn them away and of course they were right. I remember my mother asking them to sit on the back steps while she and my grandmother hustled up a plate of eggs and bacon or spam, toast from our home made bread, and a steaming cup of coffee. If Dad was home he would sit with them at the kitchen table and listen to their stories and wish them well and God's speed as they went on their way. Often they would mow the lawn or carry clinkers up from the basement furnace, and Dad would disappear into his closet and reappear with a worn wool sweater or a favorite flannel shirt to be worn under their tattered jackets."

As remembered by
Madge Sawyer
LaCrosse, Wisconsin

———————————

CHICKEN THIEVES

It was a fact of life in the 1930's, there were a lot of chicken thieves around. There was always a market for chickens and they were easy to pluck off the roosts at night in their coops without so much as a flutter of wings.

At the Stahlbusch farm in Elk Mound, Wisconsin, a part of the chicken barn had been delegated to calves one winter. When the thieves came and opened the door, a burst of penned calves came at them and out the door running wild in their new freedom. They ran out on the train tracks and stood there transfixed by the lights and train blast. Three of them were killed.

When the damage was submitted to the Railroad, the family was surprised to find they paid top dollar for the calves. With stock prices at rock bottom this was a bonanza not counted on.

MY FAMILY RECOLLECTIONS

Chapter 4

Growing Up

DID WE HAVE FUN?

Yes! When the week was over and the work was caught up we found time to have fun. House parties were in and the word went out by mid week where it would be. There was always music and the furniture was put aside so everyone could dance. If the house became too crowded as more showed up you simply stayed outside and had a good time exchanging stories and jokes. Generally the hostess had some sort of lunch like a fresh chocolate or spice cake. It didn't take much to give everyone a good time. The camaraderie was what everyone came for. It was always good to see each other again. The telephone was used for messages only; being an open line you couldn't visit much.

In the afternoons in nice weather we gathered in the neighborhood and played outside games. Flip Sticks was one of the popular games requiring only the gathering of sticks to cover holes in the ground. With a larger stronger stick the player would knock the little sticks on to the next hole. There were rules so it was a challenge to see who would win. Any number and all ages could play this game.

When you tired of the same game you could switch and play croquet without a set. You used rocks the size of an egg and the same hitting sticks to knock your rock into the next hole. It was possible to forget all about time when you played this game, often with the elders joining in. The usual large pan of popcorn followed any game.

And of course everyone had stilts. Made out of any strong

piece of wood or sticks you attached a leather made stirrup for your feet and away you went. Of course you fell a lot while practicing, but skinned knees healed and bruises faded while you kept right on practicing to be the best stilt walker around.

E. Krebs
Harlingen, Texas

FAMILY GATHERINGS

It was the custom to gather at relatives homes on Sundays where the grown-ups reviewed the situation of the country and generally had a good time. Sunday company kept families close. The children, mostly all being cousins, eagerly looked forward to the long summer and the happy gatherings.

On one particular Sunday get together five families came, each with four or five little ones, close to twenty children in all from diaper age to eleven years old.

The children were all playing in the yard and the adults, all wearing their Sunday clothes, were talking about the changes to expect when Hoover was voted out and Roosevelt would take over. In the meantime the young boys got into one of Grampa's old muskets. They were in one of the old sheds on the place and the boys were trying to fire the old gun. They opened a shot gun shell and put the powder down the musket barrel. A wad of paper was rammed down over the powder, the shots were added and more paper was pushed into the barrel. The gun didn't fire. All the boys took turns cocking the hammer and pulling the trigger while all the little kids were close around watching the performance and getting excited about this big project. One young entrepreneur solved the problem by coming up with the idea of putting a match head on the firing pin.

With the gun laying on the bench it went off like a cannon in World War I. The kids were as thrilled as if a home town ball player might have hit a home run in the World Series. They were running all over, in the house and out again, all shouting and screaming at the same time. The shocked parents were all on their feet at once running for the door to account for their own first and then to assess the situation for injuries or to determine damage.

It was all a part of the Sunday family gatherings.

P. A. Cichy
Minneapolis, Minnesota

IT MADE MEN OUT OF BOYS

Up at 12:00 midnight to pick up the daily papers, back to bed at 2:00 A M, up again at 6:30 to deliver the papers, report to serve at mass at 8:00, all on no breakfast, (you couldn't eat and go to communion) was the life of a 10 year old Catholic paper boy if you lived in the big city. You were used to it since you had started on the bottom rung at age 8.

Thirty days of this paid $4.50 which was handed over to your Mother. She always gave you a quarter for your pocket for the week and you had learned how to make it last.

If there were younger siblings in the family they were put to work as soon as they were barely able. It enabled you to take a bigger route selling considerably more papers. The little sisters were positioned at the corners of the street with a large heap of papers while you took the busy stop sign, yelling at the top of your voice, "Chronicle Examiner", or the current headlines. Cars screeched to a halt holding out the dime while you tossed papers into customers hands until the huge pile was gone. Nearby tenants came running over for a copy before they were sold out. Your pockets were full of dimes and so were the pockets of little sisters. You gathered it all together and woe to the girls if they didn't reveal a tip they might have received .

The paper delivery business usually had it's beginning with a beat up old wagon until the business grew and you could afford to buy a brand new bike on time payments. You had the world by the tail when that day arrived, and you knew it. The bike was cleaned, polished and oiled every night to be ready for the early morning. You made your payments on time because you were firmly instructed that your credit, like your name, was to be kept spotless. Any infraction of the rule and the bike would go back. It was something to be proud of, and you brought that shiny new bike indoors at night even though bike theft was unheard of in the 1930's.

If you happened to live in San Francisco you had to deal with the long Mission Hill in getting large bundles of papers into that part of the city. And you had to do it in record time. Muscular young legs would pedal furiously for speed and momentum and quickly resort to large figure eights across the road, dipping down for power to take you all the way up. You could only do this at night when the cars had settled down.

All the while you had your eye on the Western Union Telegraph job you hoped to qualify for. Barely old enough, you were first in line to apply when you heard of an opening. Dressed in gray uniform, wearing a jaunty cap,you took your job seriously, delivering at night to corporations and businesses. Being meticulously accurate with deliveries and working at record speed was necessary to allow for a few winks before it was time to get ready for school. You felt good about being trusted with responsibilities and the income you were bringing home.

Frank R.
Cornell, Wisconsin

FAMILIES WERE COMMITTED

Children grew up, survived, thrived and grew strong with the barest minimum essentials in food and clothing. But they had a home, rented or otherwise, with a pair of stable dedicated parents overseeing the enterprise. Family unity and love was in abundance and as free as the clean air they breathed. There was a solid, unspoken rule of commitment in every home. You could count on it. Family commitment was not to be compromised.

––––––––––––––––

There were twelve brothers and sisters at the Gauvin table. With the parents it made fourteen place settings. In a large family you learned to get along. Phillip Gauvin of Elmwood, Wisconsin grew up that way. He was the fourth in the family and he figured out early on that to be friendly to family and others paid off nicely. Life was hard in so many ways. Being considerate of others made it better.

As a man, this attitude led him into business with strong public contact. A restaurant and tavern combined were a natural where he and his wife could work together. Townspeople went there from early in the morning until late at night. They had to keep prices in line with what customers could afford to keep them coming. They rarely had time to sleep, but it was a living in a time when others had nothing. Who would complain of too much work.

Phillip Gauvin
Elmwood, Wisconsin

––––––––––––––––

BIG MONEY IN GOPHERS

The dry summers encouraged gopher population to the point where something had to be done about it. Crops were meager enough without heavy damage from millions of gophers.

The county decided to pay a bounty of 1¢ per tail to be brought in to the town hall. An enterprising young boy with a bike could make up to $5.00 or $6.00 a week tending to his traps twice daily. It meant getting up early to check the traps before school, and then again every night. It kept a boy very busy, but it was nice income to help the family and hopefully even have some left over for something special.

Harold Stahlbusch
Colfax, Wisconsin

PETS FILLED A NEED

When toys were scarce there were always animals or pets to give us pleasure as children and to teach responsibility. We would become very attached, and when a pet or orphaned bird died a large funeral was held by the children.

Friends were invited, a hole was dug and the biggest boy served as priest or minister. Tears were shed as wooden crosses made out of branches and old slats went up, after which everyone expected lunch. If mother didn't have anything else on hand she would fix toast with cinnamon and sugar which would make the little group of mourners feel much better.

Edith
Menomonie, Wisconsin

GOING TO THE DUMP WAS A TREAT

We never wanted to be left behind when it was time to go to the dump. Families had little to take there because everything was used to the last inch of usefulness, but we wanted an excuse to go there. Everyone but Mom and the tiny ones went on this treasure hunt.

We would look the entire place over, spending hours kicking ashes and dirt way, finding items we could make good use of.

It took my bother many trips to find all the parts to build his bicycle. A part of a doll buggy with the wicker top torn off made a nice doll bed for me. The men found all kinds of things they used in repairing machinery and such. Splatterware bowls were laying all over. You'd bring a few home for Mom or whatever other bowl or dish you could find to bring her something.

When Grandpa and Grandma got too old to live alone they brought what they needed and what the children wanted and moved in with the younger family. The rest of the household goods were hauled to the dump. The word soon went around and people started coming. But as poor as everyone was, no one wanted to be seen scavenging for cast-offs. A trip to the dump was a very private affair.

ELEVEN YEAR RITE OF PASSAGE

Most Depression children grew up fast and learned early on that everyone was expected to contribute to house and farm chores according to his ability, as age permitted. Children were proud to be considered old enough to do responsible tasks. There was no problem with self esteem, wise parents made sure of that.

It was not uncommon for an eleven year old girl to be expected to be able to catch a chicken, pluck and dress it out, and cook it. A boy of eleven was old enough to join the threshing crew with his father, which was longed for all along. But he had to keep working, just as the men did. No one sat around. Their were lots of lighter chores a boy could do, such as keeping the cold water supply where the men needed it.

Wes Schultz
Menomonie, Wisconsin

FRIENDS AND NEIGHBORS STOOD BY

Leon and Margaret Kraft of Durand, Wisconsin, had six children when hard times hit their area in the early 1930's. Suddenly there was no work for anyone. When the drought destroyed all crops there was no income for farm payments to the bank and the Krafts, along with many others, lost their farm.

Leon was a hard worker but the best he could find paid only 50¢ a day. This didn't begin to replace shoes for six lively young children. With eight around the able and a new baby on the way, the winter became bitterly hard.

The children's school teacher noticed that one boy's shoes were so badly worn they wouldn't stay on his feet anymore. When she learned of the meager income in this household she took the little boy to town one Saturday afternoon to buy him new shoes. This man has never forgotten this act of compassion and kindness shown him when the need was so dire.

Eau Galle church members heard that the Krafts were having a serious struggle on their small income, and after Mass one Sunday provided them with a bag of canned vegetables. Poor as everyone was, there was comfort in living where everyone knew everyone else and reached out to them in their need.

When Roosevelt was elected President, people began having hope. His famous "Fireside Chats" assured the people that things would be better, and before long they were.

One day the town chairman knocked on the door of the Kraft home and asked if they could use some flour. It was like an answer to prayer for this family. The man had four fifty pound bags of commodity flour for them. They could hardly believe this bonanza of good fortune was for them. The Chairman had more good news. He asked if Leon was interested in doing road work for $2.50 an hour. Roosevelt had come through on his promise all the way to Durand, Wisconsin. The Krafts still had their valued team of good work horses, and the kind man said they too were needed and there would be an hourly income for them as well.

Others in the same plight were given jobs related to road work such as crushing rocks by hand with huge mallets, etc. Much of the work done manually was dusty and dirty, but anyone given work felt it was a windfall after years of worry and doing without.

Eventually there were fifteen children born to this hard working couple. All grew up to be better citizens for having learned early to value what they had.

WE NEVER FELT POOR

"I was the youngest of twelve, born in 1929. My father had a heart attack just prior to my birth and couldn't work anymore. He died when I was four. His biggest concern was that we never felt poor. When we didn't have enough food to go around he would call us together and offer a nickel to anyone who would go without supper. Cash was paid right there. Three or four of us would always agree gladly. When we came in for supper we came in for the night, so the money never got spent. Next morning when we got downstairs he would say, 'breakfast costs a nickel today'. Only those who had gone without the night before had any money, except for the older boys who had jobs. So we never knew we didn't have enough to go around. We never felt poor.

When Father died there were still four of us boys and two girls at home. My Mom was cheated on the girl side, so she made all of us learn to tat, sew, cook, dry herbs for medicine, darn socks and everything there was to do.

I retired as a chef, but I learned far more about cooking from my Mom than I ever did in school. Today I still make everything from scratch the way she did. My only regret is that I don't have the wood stove. I learned on one and would enjoy it a lot.

We walked the railroad tracks to pick up coal that fell from the trains, picked up grain that fell on the ground at the grain elevator and bought 'culls' at the hatchery for a penny a piece which we used for meat and eggs. The chickens were fed from the grain we gathered at the elevator.

We hunted rabbits after a snowstorm with a blanket and club. When we saw tracks enter a clump of grass, but not leave, we threw the blanket over the clump and hit it with the club.

We caught literally hundreds of pigeons, raised a garden fertilized by the same chickens, and the only food we had to buy was flour and butter.

We lived near a creek, an unending source of minnows and 'crawfish'. The minnows were kept in a stock tank for about ten days, seined out, dried on a towel and shaken in salted flour, after which they were deep fried, heads, tails and all, to a crisp, tasty treat. The crawfish were boiled like lobster.

Every year we had to prowl the creek banks harvesting horseradish. We took it home, trimmed it and scrubbed it and ran it through the hand cranked meat grinder. Everyone in the house cried while that went on, but the guy on the crank (me) cried the loudest. My mother would then can it in small jars.

We had what must have been the first artificial Christmas tree ever made. It had a porcelain base with a trunk coming up from that and wire branches that folded up against the trunk when not in use. Each branch had a candle holder at the end and after it was decorated, candles were added. Then, on Christmas eve, while one older brother stood by with the water pail, my Mom would turn down the lamps, light the candles, and for three or four minutes we'd all Oh and Ah at the beauty. Then we'd blow out the candles and talk of how pretty it was. That tree was used from 1927 or 28 until 1942 when Mom died."

Carl Holland
Berlin, Wisconsin

A PENNY SAVED IS A PENNY EARNED

"When I was about eight years old", Evelyn Lett of Tomball, Texas recalls, "Mom wanted some floor wax she could only get at several stores in downtown Springfield. I was elected to do the shopping.

I walked the five miles to town to save the bus fare, and went from store to store the entire length of main street to see if I could save Mom a penny or two on the price of the wax. As it ended up, the first store was the cheapest and I saved 1 cent. I reasoned that I could also walk the five miles back home and save my mother a full 11 cents. But in the back of my mind was a great dress I had seen for myself for 25 cents. I decided that I could buy that dress using just a bit of Mom's change.

I bought the dress, but all the five miles home I worried myself sick over spending so much money on myself. Mom wasn't too mad. It turned out to be a very good dress, and I wore it until it was hopelessly outgrown."

Evelyn Lett
Tomball, Texas

7th GRADE WAS OLD ENOUGH

As soon as children were old enough to keep track of money they could work in the family business. For Martha Knutson of Scandinavia, Wisconsin, that was when she was thirteen years old and in the seventh grade. Her parents taught her how to handle their village milk delivery. Her younger sister was sent along to help her and to learn the business, too.

In a wagon or sled, every day of the year, the two little girls were up very early to deliver fresh rich Guernsey milk in glass bottles to the village residents. They couldn't waste time because school started early. They learned to dress and eat their breakfast in a hurry so they wouldn't be late even once. If it happened it was recorded on your report card.

The farm was on the edge of the village and the lights were on long before dawn. The first pails of milk came into the house as soon as they were filled. Milked by hand, of course, the fresh milk was quickly strained, poured into sparkling clean glass bottles, securely capped with paper caps, and loaded into the children's wagon or sled. Martha and little sister were on their way before dawn making their rounds. People had their empty bottles on the porch with a dime inside for each quart they wanted.

By the time Martha reached high school age the business had grown, and the little child's wagon was replaced with a used truck a younger brother drove on the deliveries. One of the best customers they had was the Academy where all the Knutson children went to school.

Martha Knutson
Scandinavia, Wisconsin

BRINGING THE COWS HOME

"Shtink Katz Berich" is what Mama called the hill. It was on the tip of a peninsula on the far edge of the farm. It was a scary place for a little boy to venture to alone in the very early morning to bring the cows home.

Legend had it that there were many skunks in and around the hill. You had to be careful. The dog came along for protection and to help with the business end of getting the cows home. But you were worried for him, too. The dog would be no match for the skunks.

The early wake up call with a no-nonsense order to bring the herd home with no loitering left no doubt in this little boy's mind that he preferred to risk being killed by the "shtink katz" rather than face the reprimand coming if he didn't do as expected.

Willfred C.
Millerville, Minnesota

BLUEBERRY HILL LOST IT'S THRILL

Marie Wapenphal Hess started life with money in the bank. Her parents wisely deposited $25 in the bank in Marie's name as they did with each child born to them. As Marie grew she was taught to add to the sum whenever she had birthday money or earned a few nickels, pennies or dimes here and there.

When she was in her teens, living in Fairchild, Wisconsin, she was aware of the blueberries which grew wild and plentiful up on a nearby hill. Marie saw an opportunity and was quick to get there in plenty of time each season. She picked hundreds of quarts of blueberries which she sold for 3 cents a quart. Frugally she added to her account until in 1929 she had $268 in the bank in her name. Then the crash came and her money was gone, along with everyone else's.

Eventually the bank returned a fraction of her savings to her, $58 in all. That shattering episode left Marie with a lifelong distrust of savings institutions.

Gordon Hess
Fairchild, Wisconsin

Much as Senior Citizens today might be wary of the banks, the banks need not worry about the Senior Citizens. Their checks are good as gold.

It had been so long since life had been normal, as it used to be. The economy was in shambles, no work available, even the weather was a disaster. There was not enough rain to germinate the seeds in the ground and little if any snow in winter.

When at long last the ecology began to right itself and rain and snow was again something you felt you could count on, people had an elated feeling of hope. It really was getting better in some ways.

Children picked up on the good spirit and enjoyed the good things nature provided. There was snow to play with in winter again and when it melted and spring thaws became a reality, Carl Holland remembers the fun it provided.

"The creek behind our house, from whence we got the crawdads, had banks six feet high, and normally it was a small creek five feet across at most. But when the snow upstream started to melt we would watch the water rise until it came over the banks. As we watched, it would creep closer and closer until our cellar filled and the cellar doors on which we used to slide disappeared. At that point we would go out on our front porch, which was on stone pillars, and the water would be covering the top step. What a grand adventure. We pretended to be on a house boat going upstream, and if you stared at the water you could imagine you felt the motion of the boat. Mom was always handy to make sure none of us was in danger of falling in. What a fun time!

When the water receded the fun was over for awhile as clean up began. All the canning jars in the basement had to be thoroughly washed with lye soap and then scalded before we could use them again. Even those memories are fond ones now."

Carl Holland
Berlin, Wisconsin

Louise Stewart of Cedar Vale, Kansas recalls, that "during the Depression my folks gave me a calf of my very own. I was so proud of my pet! When times became bad and Mom's washing machine broke down they had to sell my calf to buy a new washer. It just about broke my heart."

Prices rising
O'er the nation
Here is one
That missed inflation

Burma Shave

"I worked for a farmer for 50¢ a day. We were up at the break of day, did the chores and went out into the woods all day long, coming in just in time to do chores again. After keeping a small amount out for a little tobacco, I gave the rest of my earnings to my father who was struggling financially like everyone else was."

Ed Krebs
Harlingen, Texas

BRUSHES AND BROOMS

"During the 1930's and 40's when I was growing up on a farm in central Mississippi we made our own brooms. Broom straw, a type of tall grass, grew in large clumps on the hillsides around that part of the country. When it became dry in the fall we collected some by twisting clumps of it off until we had a big handful. The lower part of the clump was bound around with a long strip of old inner tube. (We never had a car, so I don't know where the inner tube came from.) The tops of the straw had small tendrils of softer fiber, which was the part that swept the wooden boards comprising our floors. We made several of these brooms every fall so we would have enough to last until the next fall.

We also had a broom of sorts for the yard. Around the house there was little grass, but a good supply of weeds. When we cut the weeds we brushed the clippings away with a brush, or actually, a limb from one of our plum trees.

Our peach trees provided "switches", thin branches about a couple of feet long. The threat of these switches was what helped keep my five siblings and myself in line, for they really stung when they hit the backs of our bare legs.

Toothbrushes were a luxury we couldn't afford, so we made our own. Twigs about three inches long were cut from black gum trees, then about a half inch of the bark was peeled away from one end. The exposed weed was crushed to make a brush. Baking soda and salt were our early dentifrice, later to be replaced with Dr. Lyons tooth powder.

My grandmother used one of the black gum brushes in a different way. She would wet the brush end, then "scrub" it into her container of snuff and place it in her mouth. I could never understand why she would put that stinky, ugly stuff in her mouth, and could not believe she actually enjoyed it!

Doris Dolph
Schofield, Wisconsin

Growing up in the 30's was anything but boring for a young boy. One particular young boy on the go remembers when credit wasn't so easy.

"When I started school in the first grade I stayed with my Grandmother in a little village of 124 population. Today, it is still at 124 population. My best friend was the garage man's son whose father was the best mechanic anywhere in the area. He knew everything there was to know about those early cars. But, like everyone else, he was poor too, because people just couldn't pay. When he had the customer's car running again, they all too often said "charge it". My friend heard the customers say this all the time and he well knew his father had no money to even pay his own bills.

At one end of the little town was a dance hall and speak easy where ice cream cones were also sold. My friend and I were yearning for an ice cream cone that morning and not coming up with any idea of how to earn 10¢. Finally, my friend said we could buy without money. His father's customers did it all the time. I had never heard of it, so he explained that all you do is say "charge it". So we went and ordered a cone for each of us. When the merchant asked for 10¢, I said "charge it". Well, it didn't work so slick for us. The man was not happy and said we had to pay our debts before we could buy anything more in his store."

P. A. Cichy
Minneapolis, Minnesota

Soldier, sailor
    And marine
        Now get a shave
            That's quick and clean

Burma Shave

It was this generation of children, city and country, boys and girls, who grew up to save us all.

Weary parents had given their best years to fighting the circumstances, only to find they had to send their children to fight a brutal war in lands across the seas they had never heard of. Unprovoked and without warning Japan had attacked our country on a peaceful Sunday morning in December, creating the most bitter, bloodiest fighting of all time.

Far too many did not come back but lost their lives on infested lands, dying under unbelievably inhumane conditions, or going down with their ships in shark infested seas or with their air craft, never to be heard of again.

The children of the 1930's didn't ask for anything. They grew up giving. Those that came back from the war faced a country raped of everything a land should have for it's people and ravished by war efforts that had put all mending on hold.

All too many veterans who returned died soon after, their spirits and bodies shattered, having had only the satisfaction of returning to home soil.

Others needed time to adjust. It was very hard. But there was work to be done and they set about to do it. In their life span this generation of men and women brought this country back to a record of achievement in production and growth as never before in history, at the same time giving us a trusting, honest and fair society to live in. The strength and character they developed from growing up in the Great Depression became our most valuable national resource.

Tested in peace
　　　　Proven in war
　　　　　　　Better now
　　　　　　　　　Than ever before

Burma Shave

Hindy dinky
　　　　Parley voo
　　　　　　　Cheer up face
　　　　　　　　　The war is thru

Burma Shave

Cheer up face
　　　　The war is past
　　　　　　　The "H" is out
　　　　　　　　　Of shave at last

Burma Shave

Pa likes the cream
Ma likes the jar
Both like the price
So there you are

Burma Shave

Other things have
Gone sky high
Half a dollar
Still will buy
Half pound jar

Burma Shave

She kissed the hairbrush
By mistake
She thought it was
Her husband Jake

Burma Shave

MY FAMILY RECOLLECTIONS

Chapter 5

The Earth Provided

A GARDENER

God and I once a garden made,
And how our plants grew.
I did my part with rake and spade,
He gave the sun and dew.
I thought that I was needed
For the garden we had grown,
Until I saw wild roses
That God had grown alone.

Author unknown
Submitted by
Dorothy Van Amber
Alexandria, Minnesota

THE EARTH PROVIDED

It was the custom to rely on the land to provide the healthiest foods a homemaker could prepare for her family.

There were lambsquarters early in spring and mushrooms by the pails full. Then, before the vegetable gardens produced their rich bounty, rhubarb made it's appearance and was used for succulent desserts until midsummer or later. Women knew how to cook and it had little to do with finances.

Ann Kadlecek of Phillips, Wisconsin passes on some of her finest creations which still live on in her family. Every delicious morsel was packed with natural vitamins and minerals. Even the eggs were free of any toxic material as we know them today. She writes, "The eggs and lambsquarters are something we still wait for each spring." Later in the season it can be made with spinach, beet tops, or chard, but is more delicate with lambsquarters.

Scrambled Eggs and Lambsquarters

Clean and saute lambsquarters in a little water till tender and drain. Put into fry pan with 1 to 2 tablespoons butter, lard or oil. Simmer till no liquid is left. Add eggs, salt and pepper and scramble all together till eggs are well done.

There wasn't a regular recipe but you usually had a medium bowl of greens to start with and the eggs were added to suit your taste and stretch the recipe.

Serve with hot biscuits or rolls with jelly. This was a quick, inexpensive and filling meal.

We also make mushrooms on that order, except we add caraway and onion, but also scramble raw eggs into the fried mushrooms. This mushroom dish served with home made rye bread was an extra tasty treat.

Chek Mushrooms and Eggs

Clean, wash and cut up mushrooms that are in season. Drain. Put into a heavy fry pan with 1 or 2 tablespoons lard or oil. Add 1 teaspoon caraway seed and 1 medium onion chopped. Add salt, a little water and simmer covered till tender. When tender simmer till all liquid is gone. Add as many eggs as you'd like, scramble into mushrooms and fry till done.

A favorite family dish made many times by Mrs. Marv Cartwright was hominy. It took a lot of preparation to get it ready for the jars but it was well worth it. It was popular because field corn was free for the taking. There was no market for that either. In fact, some households used it to heat their homes, kernels and all.

You could get all you wanted and with preparation it made a good and filling dish. People became so fond of it they are still using it today, and many make it themselves as they and family members before them always did. The recipe follows:

Hominy

Soak field corn in water overnight. Begin cooking corn in hot water with soda and cook about 5 1/2 hours to boil the hulls off. Add more soda and boiling water occasionally as needed. Wash to remove tip ends. The secret is, it takes an enormous amount of washing to get the hulls and tip ends all off. The soda taste also has to be rinsed off again and again and even after the jar is opened. Fill pint jars not quite half full to allow for expansion. Add boiling water to an inch or so from the top of the jars. Add 1/4 tsp. salt to each pint. Screw on rings. Cook in pressure canner 40 minutes at 10 lbs. pressure.

Mrs. Marv Cartwright
Elk Mound, Wisconsin

UNADULTERATED AND UNPOLLUTED

We consumed "earth friendly" foods without concerns about additives. No pesticides to deal with, no atrazine saturated growing medium for our vegetables and no preservative sprays needed on our food to keep it from spoiling enroute from the grower to the shelves.

Vegetable gardens were sacrosanct. We prayed for rain to soak the parched soil. A good soaking of heaven-sent warm nitrogen rich rain would save the plants. When that didn't materialize we pumped water, most often by hand, and carried it down to the garden.

Family recipes were planned heavily around the contents of these vegetable gardens with the soup pot in use regularly. In many kitchens it was always on the back burner or where it could simmer. Everything imaginable would go into it, such as all water poured off from cooking vegetables and potatoes, bones left over from slicing meat for the table, left over meat, gravy, veggies, macaroni, rice, all but sauerkraut. No salt was added because it was already in the ingredients. Pepper was used generously, along with several whole cloves and often garlic, making it a tasty, nutritious and frugal dish. It was different each time and helped satisfy the appetite to make a meager meal go farther.

If you didn't have room to grow potatoes you could buy a 100 pound burlap sack full for a dollar most anywhere.

"Ever since I was a child, my grandmother would cook this dish for me", Allison A. Bailey of Menomonie, Wisconsin remembers very well. "It quickly became my favorite dish, and I requested it frequently. My grandmother told me that her mother made this dish to feed her seven growing children. She claimed it is a dish that 'sticks to your ribs'. It is quite economical and easy to prepare. From personal experience, I suggest making it ahead so that flavors can mingle. The name of this very German meal is Bohnen Durcheinander Gekocht.

Bohnen Durcheinander Gekocht

Equal parts green beans and quartered potatoes with the skins on
(4 potatoes for 4 servings)
1 medium onion, diced
1 medium tart apple, diced
1 lb. bacon fried and crumbled (save the fat)
1 can sliced mushrooms (optional)

In large pot bring water to a boil. Add quartered potatoes,
green beans, onions, apple and mushrooms. In large skillet
cook bacon. Stir potato mixture frequently. After cooking
bacon drain between paper towels. Crunch bacon into pieces.
Add some bacon fat and all of the bacon to the potato bean
mixture. Stir and add water or pour off to about one inch.
Simmer for another 5 minutes. It is ready to serve. However,
for best results, make ahead, cover and refrigerate overnight
to allow flavors to mingle. This recipe makes 4 main dish
servings or can serve more as a side dish.

Allison A. Bailey
Menomonie, Wisconsin

Beans and Kraut

Soak one cup navy beans and cook until partially done. Add
any kind of pork, but ribs are best. Cook until almost tender.
Add 1 quart sauerkraut and cook another hour on very slow
heat. Serve with mashed potatoes.

This is the original recipe, but the same dish was prepared without meat when it wasn't available. In that case, a spoonful of bacon grease or meat drippings added flavor.

Milwaukee, Wisconsin

GRANDMA FOUND A WAY

When the family was out in the field picking potatoes or husking corn, my grandmother would leave the field early and pick up a pumpkin from the corn field. By the time father and the kids finished the job for the day and went home there was a large kettle of Pumpkin Soup and a loaf of home made bread ready for supper. There were no left overs. A smaller version of her recipe follows.

Pumpkin Soup

Heat four cups milk to boiling point. Add 1/2 teaspoon salt, 2 tablespoons sugar and 1/2 cup flour mixed with water. Cook 5 minutes. Add 1 cup mashed pumpkin, stirring in well. Add additional sugar and milk according to taste preference.

An easy way to prepare this soup is to cut the pumpkin and cook in advance. Cool, mash and store in quantities needed for soup.

Dolores Joswlak
Hatley, Wisconsin

Grandma Giovanna's Soup

At Grandma Giovanna Bertino's house in Osborn, Idaho, soup was on the noon menu every day. It was a hearty nourishing soup and everyone relished it. One old cowboy from a neighboring ranch frequently showed up at noon for a bowl or two of Grandma's soup. He would not accept anything else. He never failed to thank Grandma, telling her it was the best soup he ever ate.

In advance, boil pork, beef shank or whole chicken. Throw in a pinch of salt, a little pepper and a sprinkling of parsley. Add chopped onion, tomatoes, potatoes and rice. While simmering prepare and add carrots, beans, and seasonal vegetables. Lastly add rosemary, sweet basil and leaf of sage. Keep simmering until time to eat. Tasting is important to be sure seasoning is just right. Makes enough for 6 to 12 people.

Of course Grandma did not use a recipe. She did with what she had and could raise in her garden.

Belvena W. Bertino
Osburn, Idaho

Young beet greens with little beets left on were delicious with vinegar and a pat of butter. Vinegar was also used on fat meat and in bean soup as cooking wine is used today.

Alvina Alm
Sauk Center, Minnesota

RUSSIAN THISTLE GREENS

In north central Montana it didn't always rain either and the dry spells lasted from one season to the next. Of course our dry land gardens didn't grow but the thistles did. Mother thought we needed some greens so decided to experiment with Russian thistles. She reasoned that if fixed right they should be edible. Accordingly, she had us kids (there were plenty of us with 11 in the family) pull young thistles, six to eight inches high, by the roots rather than pick them. That way she was able to salvage more tender greens. My best rememberance is that she cooked them slightly and served them in an egg and cream sauce, something like an omelet or quiche, although I am sure she had never heard of quiche. It was edible. We ate it as often as she fixed it but never considered it a favorite. It was replaced by other greens whenever they were available.

Belvina W. Bertino
Osburn, Idaho

BOUYAH BY THE GALLON

Green Bay, Wisconsin became popular as the city of Bouyah chefs. Reputations were built on the expertise of this culinary experience. Belgian in origin, the meal soon caught on with the men's groups where fellows had the honors of preparing and serving the wholesome gourmet meal. It was intended for large gatherings and became popular with family oriented social functions. Everyone enjoyed bouyah as much as the social comaraderie that went with it. Beer barrels were brought out and tapped. Life didn't get any better after a hard week's work.

Bouyah for 75

Using a large heavy cooking vessel (heavy so it won't stick and burn), brown 5 pounds chicken cut into pieces. Then brown 2 1/2 pounds of beef cubes and 1 pound of cut up onions on low to medium heat after chicken has been removed from pot.

Add chicken to beef and cover with water adding 3/4 teaspoon pepper and 1/8 cup salt.

Cook gently until meat is tender. Remove chicken and cut into bite size pieces. Add to pot.

Add 1 pound carrots cut up fine; 10 minutes later add 1 pound celery cut fine, 1 pound cabbage shredded and 1 gallon diced potatoes. When about tender add 1 large size can (or a quart home canned) tomatoes and 1/4 cup dried or 1 cup fresh parsley.

Add water as needed to make a thick stew. Serve in bowls like chili. Makes 5 gallons which serves 75.

L. D.
Green Bay, Wisconsin

GREEN TOMATO STEW

To conserve food during the Depression, my grandmother picked all the green tomatoes before the first frost. From these she made a "green tomato stew". It wasn't quite as good as stewed red tomatoes but something you had to develop a taste for.

Stewed Tomatoes

1 quart canned tomatoes or 1 #303 size can
1 medium onion diced fine
Salt and pepper to taste
2 slices stale bread diced
Cook till onions are done. Serve hot.

R. Trudeau
Dwight, Michigan

BEANS SUSTAINED THEM

Bud Raeder remembers as a child eating well on their farm despite the lack of rain. There was beef and pork on the table. You couldn't sell the livestock. As soon as the weather cooperated his father planted lots of navy beans which survived the dry weather better than most other garden vegetables.

Bud remembers never tiring of the roaster full of sorghum and molasses laced beans his mother had in the oven most of the time. When you came home from school or work in the cold outdoors you helped yourself to a thick slice of home made bread, piled beans on it, folded it over and relished it. You didn't need anything more than that.

When it rained again times got better and Bud's family could eventually look forward to a vacation now and then. They never locked the doors when they left. Even the keys were left in the truck and car ignitions while they were gone. They didn't have to worry about things like that.

Bud Raeder
Elmwood, Wisconsin

Fourteen children to cook for plus a hard working husband was no challenge for Louise Carney of Montana. She used large pots and pans and cooked good solid food for the kids to grow on. Meal planning was automatic. Louise could do magic with potatoes. They were the life line of most dinners served in her large kitchen with sixteen gathered around the long table.

Everyone liked mashed potatoes which were served in huge bowls with navy bean soup ladled over. This was a favorite because the bean soup was flavored with bits of ham or bacon and seasoned just right. It was a dish they never tired of. Beans and potatoes were raised in large quantities to make sure the supply would not run out.

Chicken noodle soup also made a tasty topping for mashed potatoes, as well as fresh sauerkraut from the crock in the cellar.

Or, for variety, dried cod fish or tuna or hamburger could be stretched to the limit when made in milk gravy and served over mashed potatoes or bread. These were the meals Lucille craved when she was away from home for long.

Lucille Keener
Billings, Montana

FAST FOOD BEANS

Beans can be canned very easily before they are 100% dry in the garden. Pull them and put them in a pile until the pods are wilted. Then pick the beans and shell them immediately. Then they are cooked and preserved by canning in the pressure canner. No need to remember to soak beans the night before.

C. Holland

Gene's Original Kenosha Kraut

Cut up and fry 1/2 lb. salt pork. Push to side of pan and add 1 sliced onion, 3 cloves chopped garlic and 1 lb. fresh cabbage cut coarsely. Turn lightly to reduce size. Add pepper, no salt, and 2 lbs. kraut. Stir till hot and bubbly. Simmer 1 hour or more. Stir to tumble frequently. Serve with lots of whipped potatoes. Bratwurst was served with this meal when available.

Eugene Weaver
Sun Lake, Arizona

One could almost say cabbage was the most valuable vegetable to include in a garden, in spite of the fact that it took extra work to keep the butterflies and hense the cabbage worms under control. It was well worth the effort.

The season for fresh cabbage for the table was unusually long, beginning with the first small solid head for cole slaw until almost Christmas time when cabbage was still fresh in cool, dark, dirt floor cellars.

A wise gardener tried to add a few red cabbage plants to be used in fall and winter for the sweet sour cabbage dishes everyone loved. An ethnic recipe follows.

Sweet Sour Cabbage

Brown 1 med. size onion lightly in 4 T bacon fat reserved from frying 4 pieces of bacon until crisp. Add 1 medium sized red cabbage, coarsely cut. Cover and steam until done. Slice two tart apples and add to cabbage. Cook only till apples are done. Add 1/3 c brown sugar and 1/2 cup vinegar. Crumble bacon on top for garnish.

Sarma Cabbage Roll

This famous polish dish can either be baked in the oven or cooked on the stove top in a heavy pan. The head of cabbage can be either frozen the day before or cooked in a large pan of water to loosen the leaves. Left overs are as delicious as the day the dish was made and can also be frozen for future use.

Mix 1 lb. of lean ground beef and 1 lb. of ground pork with 1 lb. of ground ham or turkey sausage. Add 1 cup raw rice, 1 large grated onion, 1/2 t garlic powder or 1 grated clove, 1/2 can tomato soup (or sauce or puree), 1 T salt and 1/2 T pepper. Roll up in cabbage leaves to make uniform rolls. Place side by side. Barely cover with water, bake 1 hour at 350.

Cabbage Hotdish

Fry 1 lb. lean ground beef with 1 grated or chopped onion. Shred a head of cabbage and layer it with the cooked beef in a casserole dish. Top with 1 can tomato soup, salt and pepper. Cover. Bake 1 hr. or until cabbage is tender. Canned tomatoes can be used in place of soup, but must be drained before adding to the dish.

Fortunate was the husband from St. Paul, Minnesota who married his beautiful bride who came with a suitcase full of clothes and the following recipe for horseradish relish. She has served it with every kind of meat and after 50 years he still wants it on the table every day.

Harry and Celia Aaronson
St. Paul, Minnesota

Beet and Horseradish Relish

Cook 6 to 8 large or medium sized beets. Peel and grate as for hash browns. Combine with 1/3 c prepared horseradish. Mix together 1 t dry mustard, 1/2 t salt, 1/2 t pepper, 1 T sugar, 3 T cider vinegar, and 1 1/2 c sour cream. Add to the above and serve.

Fried Green Tomatoes

Select large green tomatoes just before they are ripe. Slice half inch thick, roll in corn meal, and saute till golden brown on each side, turning only once.

F. C.
Texas

Kraut and Dumplings

Cook 1 quart sauerkraut on low heat 30 minutes, adding 1 cup water.
Mix 1 egg yolk, 1 cup buttermilk, 1 tsp soda, 1 tsp sugar, and 1/2 cup bread crumbs. Add enough flour to make a stiff batter.
Drop into boiling kraut. Cook 12 to 15 minutes with cover on.

Cahoctus
A Russian dish by H. Crawford

Grind together 5 med sized potatoes with 1 onion.
Add salt and pepper and 1 lb. hamburger.
Add water to make it quite moist.
Bake at 325° for 2 hours or more.

WE FILLED UP ON POTATOES

We ate an awesome amount of potatoes in every size, shape and form. If we didn't have well over ten gunny sacks of potatoes stored on the cellar dirt floor we knew we'd run out before spring.

There wasn't anything better than fried potatoes, especially raw fried crisp and brown in pure lard in a cast iron fry pan. You turned them once while frying on medium heat, seasoned them at the beginning, covered them while finishing the browning on the other side. Everyone wanted seconds, that was for certain. And you served them with anything you had on hand, for any meal of the day. With eggs they were super, with cottage cheese and bread and butter pickles you thought you were in heaven.

But you prepared them lots of other ways as well. Boiled with the jackets on by the kettle full made for easy Sunday meal making or for when company stopped by. Cooking potatoes with the skins on was the secret to full flavored hash browns guests would want the secret ingredient for. Or tasty potato salad was made using a simple dressing of cream, apple cider vinegar and sugar. Mustard and hard boiled eggs added color and flavor.

Of the many ways to do potatoes the famous Polish Pieriogis stood the test of time and survived very well. Home made pasta was the principal ingredient in this dish and it took time to put it all together. It was a great meal with the little pockets filled with potatoes, cheese and seasonings. You served this with cole slaw or sweet sour beets or sauerkraut or anything else for that matter.

Almost all nationalities relied heavily on pastas, differing only in preparation and broth medium. Italians used tomatoes while the Germans and Polish used meat broth. They all made excellent filling meals so necessary for children coming home from school after miles of walking with sometimes only a lard sandwich for lunch. Husbands in from hours of hard work out in the cold took comfort in finding the kitchen elbow deep in pasta or pieriogi preparation.

Pieriogi

Stir together 3 c flour and 1 1/2 t salt in a large bowl. Beat 1 egg lightly, add 4 t oil and 3/4 c water. Add to flour mixture. Dough should be soft and not sticky. Add a tsp of water if necessary. Use a little more flour for kneading and knead until smooth. Cover for 30 minutes.

Filling:
Peel and cut 2 or 3 potatoes in cubes. Cover with water, add 1/2 t salt and cook until tender. Drain.
Melt 1 T butter and add 1 chopped onion. Cook until golden. Mash cooled potatoes. Add onion, 1 T chopped parsley, pepper, and 1 1/4 c shredded American or cheddar cheese. Add 5 T sour cream or yogurt to make a soft dough.

Divide pasta dough into 4 parts. Keep remaining dough covered while you roll out one fourth at a time as thin as possible. Cut in rounds with a glass, place heaping teaspoon of filling in center, fold over and pinch shut securely.

Cook in gently boiling water with 1/2 t salt added. Cook a dozen at a time in a wide pan. When they come up cook a bit longer, about 5 or 6 minutes until done. Drain well. Keep warm in a warmed dish in the oven as you cook the batches. Serve with hot butter sauce.

Butter sauce:
Saute onions in melted butter and pour over dish. Makes 4 dozen pieriogis. Left overs can be fried for another meal.

Crispy Fried Potatoes

Peel potatoes (new ones do not need to be peeled) and slice into a large bowl. Combine some flour and salt and sift over sliced potatoes, mixing well. Turn into preheated pan using lard or oil for frying. Brown on one side, turn and cover to brown on other side.

Julie Richter
St. Paul, Minnesota

POTATO PANCAKES

"Potato pancakes were not as easy to make in my mother's day," *Adeline Dietsche of Wausau, Wisconsin* remembers. "Mother didn't have a blender and we had to grate the potatoes on a hand grater which many times meant skinned knuckles.

We had a large family so that meant many potatoes to grate. We all liked potato pancakes. Simple to make, Mother would add some flour, milk and eggs until it was the consistency for frying. We fried them in a large black cast iron fry pan and we would make a complete dinner of the pancakes.

We ate them with Karo syrup or usually with just sugar sprinkled on. We also had home canned apple sauce to serve with them. The combination is still one of my favorite meals."

Mother's Potato Pancakes

3 c grated potatoes (onion is optional)
2 eggs
Approximately 1/2 c flour
1 t salt
2 T milk

Fry in lard or bacon grease.

Potato Balls (Dumplings)
To be served with meat or foul.

Pass 9 medium size boiled potatoes, 9 slices stale bread and 1 large bunch parsley through food chopper. Add 6 eggs, salt and pepper to taste, and 2 1/4 cups flour.

Cut 2 slices bread into small cubes and fry in butter until light brown; add to above mixture.

Form into small balls (size of golf balls or smaller) and place in refrigerator until needed.

Just before serving time drop potato balls into boiling salted water. When they rise to the surface (only a few minutes) they are done. 10 to 12 servings.

Mrs. Paul Kircher
Oshkosh, Wisconsin

Komle (Potato Balls)

4 c grated raw potatoes
1 t baking powder
1 t salt
1 c white flour

Drain any liquid from potatoes. Combine ingredients and work lightly into dough. Shape by hand into balls or dumpling shapes. Drop into broth made from ham, pork roast, or pork hocks. Cook for 1 hour.

Deloris Nelson
Verona, Wisconsin

FOURTH OF JULY GERMAN POTATO SALAD

Paula Schmidt vividly recalls this holiday celebrated as a family picnic when she was a child.

"As I was growing up in the 1930's I always remember the Fourth of July as a sunny, warm day spent outside. You realize that there were probably also lousy Fourth of July days, but my memory has conveniently deleted the clouds, cold, wind, rain, etc.

To keep all the feuding relatives on the best behavior my mother usually had the annual picnic for some twenty people. It was outside in the back yard near the pear tree on a large trestle table my father would concoct of 'savings' of lumber and saw horses he'd hoarded in the garage.

Mother and Mrs. Hereth, our housekeeper, spent the day of July third making the German Potato Salad, my father's mother's recipe. Both Mom and Mrs. Hereth grumbled in the kitchen as they cooked the new potatoes and peeled them. If they'd catch me I'd have to help with the peeling and slicing.

I don't remember much of what we ate that day, only the time and effort and mumbles that went into the potato salad. The recipe that follows is scaled down to family size, or a fraction of what was made for the 4th of July dinners."

German Potato Salad

Peel & slice 6 boiled potatoes (new or red potatoes don't fall apart). Meanwhile fry 1/4 lb. bacon until crisp.
Boil 2 eggs firm, chop whites and add to sliced potatoes.
In pan with some bacon fat left in add:
1/2 c water
1/2 c vinegar
1 T flour (or more to slightly thicken)
1/2 to 1 t sugar
1 t dry mustard
1/8 t pepper & 1 t salt
Cook until liquid is somewhat absorbed and has a glassy look.
Add to potatoes along with crumbled bacon and egg yolk.
Use sieve with remaining yolks to decorate.
Can be served warm or cold.

"It was heated the next day on top of the gas oven as the oven was used for other parts of the picnic feast."

Paula Schmidt
Wausau, Wisconsin

CRACKLINGS ADDED FLAVOR AND CRUNCH

Helen Tambornino, of Wausau, Wisconsin, knows how it was done. "To render lard, the fat from pork was first put through the meat grinder and then heated on the stove. It took almost continuous stirring to keep the lard from burning. The lard was snow white after it was cooled. The lard would be poured into earthen jars and would keep indefinitely.

The cracklings that were left over from the lard were golden brown and tasted much like bacon. They were often used to make corn bread. They also found their way into soups and many other recipes. Any cracklings not used for cooking were fed to chickens and pigs.

Crackling Potatoes

Slice potatoes, fry together with cracklings and onion. Stir often while frying.

Helen Tambornino
Wausau, Wisconsin

Hasty Creamed Potatoes

Cut peeled raw potatoes into slices or cubes. Season with salt and pepper. Put in a pan with a pat of butter. Cover with milk. Cook over low heat till done. They make their own starch for thickening.

THE IRISH HAD A WAY WITH FOOD

Every nationality had their favorite "cheap food". Most of the skill in preparation was brought over from the old country. The foods were usually made out of the most inexpensive commodities available to the area.

Women became very talented at concocting these dishes which were always big favorites because the families grew up on them. They instinctively knew the very touch of a specific spice or herb the dish called for. Even when times changed and progress made it easier and quicker for the homemaker to prepare meals for a family, these dishes stayed popular when times got hard in the bitter, dirty 30's. They provided good satisfying food.

Potatoes were definitely a standby food for the Irish. There were the Irish potatoes, small and cream colored which made the best country fries or raw fries anyone could dream of. Using bacon for flavor made it a meal.

This recipe for potatoes and cabbage was handed down in the Johanna youngerman family of Menominee, Michigan.

Calcannon

Bring a pot of salted water to boil and boil 1 medium sized cored and quartered head of cabbage until tender, 12 to 15 minutes. Drain off water, chop cabbage and set aside. In another pot of water boil 2 lbs. of scrubbed, unpeeled, sliced potatoes. Drain and set aside. Put 2 chopped leeks into sauce pan, add 1 cup milk, and simmer until tender.

Add to potatoes 1 1/2 Tbsp. mace, salt and pepper, and 2 garlic cloves, minced. Mash with hand masher.

Add leeks and milk. Mix and mash in cabbage and lastly 1 stick unsalted butter. Transfer to oven proof dish and place under broiler to brown.

Corned Beef Dinner

Place 3 to 4 lbs. corn beef round in Dutch oven and barely cover with water. Add 2 sliced onions, 2 minced garlic cloves, and 2 bay leaves. Cover and simmer (do not boil) 1 hour per lb. of meat. Remove meat from broth and add 6 small peeled potatoes and 6 small carrots. Cover and cook 10 minutes. Then add 1 medium head cabbage cut into wedges. Cook 20 minutes longer or until vegetables are done. To carve corned beef, cut at a slight angle across the grain making thin slices.

No Irish dinner is quite complete without the traditional

Soda Bread

Into a large bowl mix 5 1/4 cups flour with 1 tsp soda and 1 tsp salt. Make a well in the center and pour into it 1 1/2 cups buttermilk (or fresh milk with 1 tsp cream of tartar). Knead dough swiftly and lightly into a ball. Dough should be soft so may need a bit more liquid. Flatten the ball with well floured hands. Place on greased baking sheet. Make a cross on top. Bake at 400 degrees 45 minutes for one large loaf, 30 to 35 minutes for 2 small loaves. Eat hot or cold. Store leftover bread in a tea towel to keep it soft.

J. M. Youngerman
Menominee, Michigan

WPA Soup

6 qts. water
2 c celery, chopped
2 c onions, chopped
2 c potatoes, chopped
2 c salami or summer sausage, cut into chunks
2 to 3 t butter
Salt and Pepper
2 eggs, whipped

In a large pot bring water to a boil. Add all ingredients except eggs and simmer for 1 hour. Blend in whipped eggs and boil for one minute. Let soup chill for 8 hours or overnight to enhance flavor. Heat and serve.

Green Bean Soup

1 qt green beans, cut into 1 inch pieces
1 to 2 c carrots and potatoes
Onion
Celery
Salt and pepper to taste
3 T vinegar
1/4 t sugar
Dash of cinnamon
2 T flour
Shortening to brown flour

Combine first 5 ingredients and cook until tender. Add vinegar, sugar and cinnamon. Make a gravy out of flour and shortening and add to soup.

Learn-a-lot Homemakers
Shawano, Wisconsin

ROCK HARD PEARS MADE EDIBLE

"In our family the boys had to help out in the kitchen, too, so two recipes will always stay with me. When my parents purchased their property in 1920 a row of fruit trees had been planted with a cherry, two apples, and a pear tree as well as several hills of rhubarb," John Cline remembers from his childhood. "The pear was a late ripening variety and while we waited until after a heavy frost to pick them they were still as hard as rocks. Wrapping them in paper and putting them in the fruit cellar helped. But they seemed to go from hard to mush overnight and had to be discarded. We also tried boiling, baking and frying but they stayed as tasteless as grass.

Mother eventually came up with a way to prepare them so all could enjoy them. They were impossible to peel so with a sharp butcher knife and muscle power we quartered them and cut out the core. We ground them in the food grinder with one boy turning the handle while the other pushed the pears down.

One of the apple trees was a yellow transparent, an early ripener, but by frost the apples were over ripe so these were peeled and quartered.

About equal quantities of both fruits were put into a large pot with a little water, brought to a boil and were simmered until the pears were soft. Using only a little sugar, the apples provided the sweetness and flavor while the pears gave the sauce body. We had a combination that could either be canned or used over biscuits or an unfrosted cake.

The hills of rhubarb were the green variety and sour as all get out. To make a decent tasting sauce took as much sugar as fruit, but in our house sugar wasn't too plentiful so we had to improvise. Up in the next block was a mulberry tree with berries the size of a thumb but tasteless as straw when ripe. Blending the two together in equal quantities and simmering in a little water produced a reasonably good sauce.

My father always asked for a rhubarb pie but my poor Mother did not have a pie pan, so she rolled out the dough and then rolled the rhubarb in it. It was baked and sliced like bread. We loved it and thought our Mother was so smart we even bragged about it to our friends."

John Cline
Wausau, Wisconsin

WE HAD FLOWERS

"Growing up in the Depression was not easy, and in our case with two parents and five children in a small house cooperation was a must. One of my younger sisters had asthma so house plants with their pollen were out of the question.

Since they did not require sunlight we could grow salt flowers and thereby decorate an area where living plants were not allowed.

To start find a shallow platter or dish. Grease the edges with petroleum jelly to keep the growth inside. Fill dish with porous rock, coal, or a piece of brick. Sprinkle on the growth medium consisting of 2 Tbsp. salt, 2 Tbsp. bluing, and 2 Tbsp. water mixed together.

Sprinkle a few drops of coloring in various places. This could be mercurochrome for red, black or blue ink, or food coloring.

In a few days you will notice salt crystals starting to form on the rock. They will grow several inches, with a variety of color if the medium is kept wet. Add 2 Tbsp. salt as the growth slows down."

John Cline
Wausau, Wisconsin

Farm and garden seed was always home grown. Even though a packet had a good measure of seed and was only 10¢, you could save quite a bit by gathering your own in the fall. Selecting the best plants and marking them made sure the next years garden would be as good as the last. You were sure to have all the seed you needed in spring when the ground was warm and ready.

H. Stahlbusch
Colfax, Wisconsin

BUNNY GUARD

A homemade spray can be made to guard your veggies from the rabbits who roam at night. After a rain spray the garden with a mixture of 1 Tbsp. Tobasco sauce and 1 Tbsp. Elmers glue mixed in a cup of water. Pour into a spray bottle. Fill with water and spray your garden before the rabbits get there.

OR
Pick up hair sweeping from the beauty or barber shop and sprinkle around the plants, or around the edge of the garden. It lasts quite a while.

OR
Cut up an old green garden hose. Lay it around to look like snakes. Rabbits and snakes don't mix.

JAPANESE BEETLES A PROBLEM?

They bring their own antidote with them. Simply take a handful, squash them and mix well with water. Pour over affected areas. It really works.

HOW TO SAVE CABBAGE WHEN IT BURSTS

Shred or cut the cabbage very fine. Mix salt into it to suit your taste. Add 2 Tbsp. sugar to each gallon shredded. Pack in jars as tightly as possible. Put rings on jars and lay the lids on top. Leave the jars at room temperature for 3 days. Seal tight and store. If some juice seeps out, it's O K. Makes very nice kraut the easy way.

P. H.
Ohio

COUNTRY PUFF-BALL MUSHROOMS

They grew in the night by the hundreds in all sizes, some like a grapefruit. They were white and solid and smelled of the earth they so quickly sprang from.

We took a pail along when we brought the cows home in the early morning. We gathered them before the sun had a chance to destroy them. Thick slices were fried in butter to surround the scrambled eggs we enjoyed for breakfast after chores. But we also used them in sandwiches and with noodles for a main dish.

R. V.

EGG STRETCH

For two servings, beat together 1 egg, 2 T milk, 1/2 C bread crumbs, salt and pepper. Fry in patties until brown on both sides.

WE ALL HAD COTTAGE CHEESE

Mom made our cottage cheese. One of the happiest sights we'd see was a pillow case hanging on the line with whey dripping in the dish pan. Not only did we enjoy the cheese but we had pancakes from the whey that I thought was better than buttermilk cakes. Lots of people fed the whey to the chickens, but not in our household.

C. Holland

ENTERTAINMENT

While money was not to be had for outside entertainment, excellent listening was available through the radio. We had marvelous music by famous orchestras such as the A & P Gypsies, Wayne King, Bing Crosby with John Scott Trotter and many more. We enjoyed the talents of gifted singers such as James Melton, Lanny Ross, Jessica Dragonette, Jane Froman, Grace Moore, Gene Autry, Rudy Valee, Billy Jones,

Ernie Hare, Perry Como, Frank Crummet and Julia Sanderson. How sad what has happened to music today.

We also had Arthur Godfrey, Al Jolson, Eddy Cantor and there were Fibber McGee and Molly, Amos and Andy, The Goldbergs, the Lone Ranger and many excellent dramatic programs.

Doris M. Fee
Hillsdale, New Jersey

SWEET MEMORIES OF MARSHMALLOWS

Evelyn Lett of Tomball, Texas knew the value of a nickel. She generously shares with us, "I was born in Springfield, Massachusetts and lived on the airport. It is no longer there but my Dad was learning to be an aircraft mechanic. He worked for free most of the time for Gee Bee Racing Co., then tried his hand at having his own shop. Times were really hard. How Mom and Dad ever made it, I'll never know.

I was eight or nine one Mother's Day and money was almost not to be had. Somehow my Dad managed to come up with a nickel. I walked more than three miles each way to find just the right gift. It had to be the most I could get for 5 cents. I finally settled for a box of marshmallows. The box at that time had 16 large marshmallows in it. I wrapped them up pretty, picked some wild flowers and gave the gift to Mom. She was so touched, she never forgot that present and spoke of it for years. After a time the presents got bigger and more expensive but Mom always got pleasure out of remembering that special gift. To this day I always include some marshmallows in her gifts."

MY FAMILY FAVORITES

Chapter 6

Their Work
Was
Cut Out For Them

WOMEN HELD IT TOGETHER

Feeding a family was no small achievement on 75¢ a day wages. It took incredible skill to come up with enough of everything to meet the needs of the family. To fill their tummies up at mealtime, plus arranging for lunches for school, the job site or the fields and woods, was enough to test the most creative cooks.

Marv Cartwright of Elk Mound, Wisconsin, came from such a family and his mother is one of those that deserves accolades for her management of her home and vegetable garden.

Marv's father was a hard worker and he was efficient, being able to do about anything that came along. He earned 75¢ a day when he could find work. If nothing else, he worked for a side of beef which worked out well for the farmer too since there was no market for livestock. Mrs. Cartwright could make a side of beef go a long way. Much of it was canned, boiling it 60 minutes or more in the hot water bath method. It was preserved in 2 quart size jars and made delicious meals with lots of natural gravy which usually was served with huge bowls of boiled potatoes. Those life sustaining, versatile potatoes rounded out many a meal at their house.

A cow was loaned to the family as the owner didn't have enough hay to keep his cows fed. The loaned cow was a life saver, providing milk, butter, cottage cheese and sour milk and buttermilk for baking pancakes and cakes. The flakiest biscuits were made using buttermilk.

And there were chickens and eggs. When the price of eggs dropped to nothing the family consumed them all themselves rather than selling any, frying a dozen at a time in fry pans large enough to meet the needs of the family. When chickens could lay no longer they were butchered and used for chicken and dumpling dinners. This meal was universally one of the best for its satisfying delicious flavor and filling quality. If you needed more you simply used a larger pan and made more dumplings. The secret to it's delectable flavor was the age of the chicken. If the chicken was canned you had a quick meal with all the tasty gravy anyone could wish for.

The children early on found whatever work they could find and came home with the money. Often they were offered a meal where they worked and that lightened the load at home. Marv was allowed to keep a little of his earnings and he learned to handle his nickels and dimes wisely, most often saving them.

When he was fourteen years old he had a full dollar, and he came to like the feeling of having money. But the day came when he had a toothache. He kept it to himself for a while but finally the pain became so intense he had to do something, and that would cost him money. He took his dollar and walked to town where the dentist took the inflamed tooth out. All the while Marv worried about the cost of all this when he had only one dollar. But the dentist looked him straight in the eye and told him the charges were a dollar. Marv was elated and relieved and couldn't wait to get home with the good news. He knew his father would have been upset had the bill been more and part of it would have been unpaid. You didn't make a debt. But from that time on his father took care of these matters himself. He pried the bad teeth out by the roots with his jack knife.

In fact, he got to be quite efficient at taking care of the children's injuries and aches and pains. When Marv stepped on an exceptionally sharp piece of glass and cut himself severely, father knew just what to do. He poured turpentine all the way into the deep cut and that took care of that. It healed without a problem.

Sometimes a member of the family would get a sore leg. If it was an adult it was called rheumatism. In a child it was growing pains, but it was treated the same. You rubbed it down well with turpentine.

In all his growing up years Marv had never been to a doctor. It was an experience waiting for him when he entered the service of his country. He fought in World War II, one of the bloodiest wars this country has ever suffered.

Marv Cartwright
Elk Mound, Wisconsin

A country wife took on a big responsibility. Arranging for meals was a year round preparation. There was no such thing as going to the grocery store on a moments notice to get something to cook for that meal. Money was tight and even gasoline for the car couldn't be used frivolously. The cellar had to be well stocked. Everything possible was raised in the vegetable garden, picked along the roadside, the edges of the fields and in the woods to provide food for the coming months ahead.

To survive, farmers shared work and machinery. Consequently there were often extra hands to prepare meals for. The ultimate challenge was cooking for the grain threshing crew. A group of twenty or more strapping hungry farmers would descend on a place at a time, sometimes with short notice of their arrival. It would take a good supply of nutritious food, ready and hot at noon to keep them all satisfied. That is, until mid-afternoon when gallons of fresh egg coffee with baskets of sandwiches and doughnuts had to be carried to the field, along with a cream can of freshly pumped cold well water.

You had to know how to organize a kitchen to keep this up sometimes for several days on a very limited budget.

Joyce Gannon and Lorraine Post of Cadott, Wisconsin, will never forget those hot summer days, rising with the sun and working over balky wood stoves. They recall that if you didn't bake pies for the threshing crews, you could kiss your reputation as a good cook good-bye. That meant six or seven pies, because any man would eat two pieces. "Those men were hungry," they recall. "They had gotten up early, done their chores at home and then harnessed the teams of horses for threshing. You had to have quite a number of teams because you couldn't let the machine stand idle. And when the men were fed and left for the fields again, there were the dishes to do, lots and lots of them."

TWO CHICKENS IN EVERY POT

The Williams Family Grocery of Menomonie, Wisconsin, did their part in an effort to fulfill President Herbert Hoover's promise to the people through the Great Depression. "A car in every garage" he had said. They couldn't provide that, but "two chickens in every pot" was their area of expertise. They could do something about that.

The Williams Family Grocery in the 1930's operated in a 5000 square foot building at the corner of 9th and Main Street. In Depression days there were only basics to choose from on the shelves. Times were very hard and few could afford anything more than essentials. To provide this for the community the grocer spent long hours supplying foods and keeping them fresh, keeping waste to a minimum, and canning anything that would spoil for home use.

Grocers then sold most of the merchandise on credit. Some customers had a hard time paying every month and got behind; a few went months and years behind and some never did get caught up.

Don recalls his memories. "We had hitching posts in front of the store. We bought live chickens from the farmers and fed them until they were ready for butchering. Then we'd butcher them on Friday to have ready in the coolers for Saturday's shoppers, the day most shopping was done. Orders were delivered through the week with a panel truck. Father had a farm and raised livestock so we'd go out there and select a choice animal, butcher it, cut it up and bring it in to sell in the meat department. It was always the freshest meat from the most select organically fed animals. We all worked together to make the business the success it was. Even the family dog had to earn his keep being in charge of the security system, his sole duty. He slept in the store every night and protected the business with the obligation of a guard dog. He earned his keep very well."

Their family business is still in operation today, now known as Don's Super Value and located in a 37,000 square foot building on downtown Broadway, where they house an awesome array of thousands of different food items.

The survival skills learned during the Great Depression served to prosper that generation when times became better. They never forgot the lessons of saving and building security into their lives, and applied them to the new healthy economy. President Clinton referred to these survivors in his 1995 State of the Union message as "the strongest generation of citizens this country has thus far known." We have much to learn from them.

Chicken Bouillon

3 to 4 lb. stewing chicken cut into small pieces.

10 chicken feet, scalded, skin and nails removed by pouring boiling water over.

Add 3 to 4 quarts boiling water.

2 stalks celery or celery root, 1 sliced onion, 1 T salt, 1/4 t pepper, 1/8 t nutmeg.

Simmer about 3 hours. Remove chicken, strain and refrigerate.

Can be used for soup, hot dishes, gravy, etc.

Chicken Soup

Stewing chicken is best, but chicken pieces for frying can be used.

1 to 2 lbs. of meat with bone.

1 sliced onion, 1 T parsley, 2 stalks celery, 1 c sliced carrots.

Cook for 45 minutes.

Remove chicken, cool and cut into small pieces, removing bones.

To broth add 1/3 c rice, 1 t salt, 1/4 t pepper, and 4 whole cloves.

Simmer until tender. Add 1/4 c small noodles if a thicker soup is desired.

Add chicken pieces. Serve hot.

Ham Squares

1 1/2 lbs. ground ham
1 lb. ground pork
3/4 c day old bread
1/3 c onion chopped
3 eggs, beaten
1/2 t dry mustard

Mix all together and spread in shallow 8 x 12 pan.
Bake 350° 1 1/4 hr.
Cover with topping of 1 c applesauce flavored with cinnamon
and red coloring.

Baked Pork Chops

Brown chops well. Place in casserole and cover with
mushroom soup. Bake 3/4 hour. Serve gravy with whipped
potatoes.

Ground Beef in Cabbage Leaves

1 lb. beef
salt and pepper
Juice of 1 med. onion
1/2 c cooked rice
2 c tomatoes
2 T vinegar
2 T sugar

Mix above together.
Soak about 8 cabbage leaves in hot water.
Roll meat mixture in cabbage leaves.
Place in heavy fry pan. Add a little water.
Simmer until cabbage is tender and well browned.

Pie Crust for Salmon or Pork Pie or Pasties

To 1 1/2 c shortening add 2 T milk, 2 t salt, 1/2 c boiling water. Whip until like whipped cream. Stir in 4 c flour, finish blending by using fingers. Shape into 4 balls. Enough for two top crusted pies.

Pork Pie

Cook 4 lbs. ground lean pork and 1 t salt in 1 qt. water for 20 minutes.

In heavy sauce pan brown 2 med. onions chopped fine.

Add ground meat and 1 c broth, made from cooking bones of pork from the butcher. Add more as needed, simmer meat until it loses all pink color. Drain and cool pork.

Add to 4 c cooked and mashed potatoes to which has been added 2 T butter, salt and pepper.

Spoon into bottom crust, add top crust, brush with milk.

Bake 400° for 10 minutes and finish 350° for another 30 minutes or until nicely browned.

Can be frozen unbaked. Bake unthawed an hour at 350°

R. Trudeau

"Something that has always fascinated me is the way poor people, or should we say the economically challenged, of various cultures used the same basic foods to keep their families fed, with their own ethnic twists to suit their food tastes. For example, my Norwegian Grandmother made her 'fried bread' for the children's snack, and topped them with clabbered cream, cinnamon and sugar, while my cousins Italian Grandmother turned hers into the original pizzas with leftover spaghetti sauce and cheese.

Also, we ate salt cod fish soaked and cooked, with melted butter on Christmas eve, while they ate theirs with olive oil, garlic and crushed red pepper. Potatoes of course were everyone's favorite."

Penny Kortus
Baraboo, Wisconsin

EARTH MEALS

"I can remember my mother sending us out in the pasture to find tree roots to make a fire burn hotter so she could bake bread. There were ten of us and she baked six loaves at a time.

She usually would have fresh bread waiting for us when we would come home from picking raspberries. My sister and I would go to one woods in the forenoon and each of us would pick a gallon and a half full. Then, if it was a nice day we'd go back and pick 6 quarts more in the afternoon. Sometimes she'd trade some with a neighbor for rhubarb or sell them to some men working on the road. But the berries sure were good on that fresh bread.

We always had a big garden that kept us all busy weeding

and hoeing. We would carry the water from the wash tubs out to the plants. The soapy water from the wash machine had to go on the onions and cabbages. Mom said this would keep the worms off. She made the cabbage into sauerkraut when the heads got firm and big."

Muriel Berghammer
Wausau, Wisconsin

Quick and Easy Kraut

"Mother would shred it with a cabbage slicer and each time she had 5 pounds shredded, 3 1/3 T of salt were added. It was packed firmly in a 10 gallon crock until it was 3/4 full, then covered with a heavy plate. A heavy stone was added and a white cotton dish cloth covered it. In about a month it was ready to use. The crock was kept at room temperature until the kraut was ready, then was transferred to the cool cellar."

One of the dishes Muriel's mother prepared from the fresh kraut was a casserole which was exceptionally tasty.

Kraut Casserole

In a 2 qt. greased casserole dish, slice a layer of potatoes and 1/2 c sliced onion. Use about 5 medium potatoes in all. Layer over it 1 1/2 lbs. extra lean ground beef. Cover with 2 c rinsed sauerkraut. Pour a white sauce over it. I use cream of mushroom soup. Bake 1 1/2 hours at 350°.

Kraut Ranza

Filling: Fry 6 to 8 slices of bacon until cooked but not crisp. (You can also use ham.)

Remove from pan, cut in small pieces and reserve. Pour off excess drippings and reserve.

Add to pan with remaining drippings, 1 qt. well drained sauerkraut, 1 large onion diced and about 1/4 head of cabbage, shredded and seasoned with onion salt and pepper.

Cover pan and cook slowly until kraut and vegetables are wilted.

Add more drippings as necessary to keep from becoming brown.

Add bacon pieces and cool.

Use your favorite dinner roll or bread dough recipe. Roll out as for cinnamon rolls. Cut in squares.

Spoon several spoonfuls of the kraut mixture on each square. Seal by pinching into pillow shapes or any way desired.

Place on greased cooky sheet, leaving space to brown all the way around. Let rise, bake as you would rolls.

Mary Webb

Beef and Kraut Dinner

Simmer slowly 2 qts. sauerkraut for an hour.

Mix meat balls as follows:
To 1 lb. ground beef and 1/2 lb. ground pork, add 1 1/2 cups soft bread crumbs to which 1/3 cup milk has been added.

Add 1/4 cup grated onion and 1 T vinegar, 1 t salt, 1/4 t pepper, and 1 egg. Form into meat balls and brown in fry pan.

Add to kraut and simmer 1 hour, adding water as needed.

Add 2 or 3 peeled and grated potatoes 15 minutes before serving.

Serve hot garnished with parsley.

YOU HAD TO HAVE YOUR HEAD ON STRAIGHT

"I never knew tender beef steak until I grew up and left home. We only butchered the oldest cow in the herd, the one that had produced calves and milk for many years. When the old cow wasn't productive anymore, and of course there was no market for them, you had beef for the table.

Young beef were a cash crop you counted on for very important things. You didn't butcher them. But when the tough old cow was butchered, dressed out and brought into

150

the house, Mother knew exactly how to handle it. Cold pack canning it with 60 minutes or more of boiling hot water bath tenderized it and took care of most of it.

Then there was the sausage. The meat was ground up by hand. It took a well calloused palm to withstand the heavy grinding of this beef. It was seasoned to perfection and stuffed with a sausage stuffer into casings. These came from the intestines of the animal, having been scraped and turned inside out, then scraped again very thoroughly and turned again. It was scraped with a short blunt knife until it was paper thin. It made excellent edible sausage casings which no substitute thus far can match in flavor or texture."

Delectable Mutton Roast

Some members of the family raised large flocks of sheep and mutton was used a great deal for meat. Unless the animal is butchered correctly and the meat cooked right, a good many people will not eat mutton. Betty Sheehan Vaira's roast mutton was so delicious it was even mistaken for beef.

Select a chunk of meat the size desired for a roast. Cut off all fat. Coat completely with apple sauce and roast until about half done. Remove all applesauce and finish roasting. Superb flavor and taste.

Belvino Bertino
Osburn, Idaho

Absolutely Delicious Venison Roast

Wrap bacon all around roast and a few pieces over it. Roast in uncovered roaster using very slow oven, 225° to 250°, for 3 hours. Be sure to make a gravy since it will be beyond words for flavor. Your guests will come back for thirds.

Carl Holland

Fried Rabbit

After rabbit has been dressed and cut into pieces for frying, soak in salt water overnight. Use 1 T salt to 1 qt. water.

Remove from water and pat dry. Coat pieces with flour after adding pepper.

Place into a hot skillet containing 1/4 cup butter or lard. Cover and fry on medium heat until golden brown, turning frequently.

To make gravy, remove meat from pan and keep warm.

Add 1 T flour into hot skillet, stir to brown lightly, add 1 cup cold water gradually, stirring continuously.

Bring to a boil and cook 1 minute. Season to taste.

Another Favorite

Cut dressed out rabbit into serving pieces. Season with salt and pepper and dredge with flour.

Fry in lard or butter until brown. Transfer to a roaster and bake 1 hour on medium heat, adding 1/4 cup water.

OR:

Pour 1/2 cup of cream over and bake as above.

Make gravy out of the drippings by adding a cup of broth or water to the pan after removing the meat.

Mix 1 1/2 T flour with water and add to the boiling broth, stirring till smooth and thickened.

A soup to warm the vitals of anyone in the coldest part of winter is Sturgeon Head Soup. A flavor all it's own, once enjoyed, you'll never forget it and will find pleasure in the long preparation of this succulent fare.

Sturgeon Head Soup

"I used to think it was my great skill that brought people to my door with their Sturgeon heads, but lately I have gained a little common sense and realize they bring them to me to avoid the mess," surmises Carl Holland, an expert in preparing this rare and sumptuous treat.

First, immerse the head in warm water with a little vinegar added to it. Scrub thoroughly with an abrasive pad. Don't use anything metallic on it. When it is washed very well, cover the head with boiling water. I use a canner for this because I usually prepare two at a time. Bring to a boil, cover, and simmer until the plates on the top start to loosen, usually about 45 minutes. Lift out and put into a clean sink to cool to the point where you can handle it. Discard the cooking water.

Now begin taking the plates and bones apart. When you come to a good solid piece of meat, set it aside. If there is fat on the meat, cut it off and throw it away. That's what gives it the fishy taste. You will get about 1 1/2 lbs. to 2 lbs. of cooked meat from each head. From there on, you're home free.

Dice potatoes and onions (add carrots if you like the color) and boil in a good chicken stock or any other meat stock you have handy. If you have any gravy or meat sauce (not tomato) add it with the stock. Chicken bouillon will work too or even water if you lack the stock. Dice the meat and add it, then when everything is tender and the liquid in the pan just covers the goodies, mix flour in enough milk to give you a good rich soup, add to the pot and cook and stir until it thickens. *DO NOT BOIL AFTER YOU ADD THE MILK MIXTURE.* Keep it just below the boiling point. Salt to taste and add all the pepper your family can enjoy. I like it to warm me as it goes down. After all, it is February when you do this. The meat from the head tastes better to me than any other part. I serve it with my home made multi grain/ cracked wheat/ whole wheat sesame roll. Lay a large sprig of parsley in the center of each bowl and sprinkle a halo of paprika around it. Your guests will KNOW they are "company".

Carl Holland

When boiling eggs, salt the water heavily; 2 or 3 T salt prevents the white from running all over should any crack.

Carl

Scrambled Potatoes

When frying potatoes and there isn't quite enough to go around add a few eggs after browning the potatoes, as many as needed. Season with salt and pepper and serve hot. Delicious for a quick meal.

Egg Grab

Yes, there was "fast food" then too. When you had a very busy day, which was much of the time, you needed something filling, good to eat and as soon as possible, even though there wasn't much of anything around to make a meal with. You had a few meals cataloged in your mind for these occasions. Egg Grab was a favorite.

Boil a large pan of peeled potatoes while you proceed with the topping.

Heat a large fry pan with 1 T of bacon drippings or butter.

Break as many eggs into a bowl as you'll need for the number of hungry people you are planning for.

Mix in flour and whole milk, or any milk for that matter.

Add salt and pepper, mix with eggs and fry until done. It will be nice and juicy.

Ladle over potatoes.

Pearl Severson
Glenwood City, Wisconsin

Delicious Left Over Rice

2 c boiled rice, 1 c canned tomatoes, 1/4 t salt, 1/4 t curry or 1/2 t turmeric, pepper. Simmer till juice is almost absorbed. Add 1/2 cup grated cheese and allow it to melt. Serve hot.

F. W.
Kansas

Tasty Meat and Potato Dish

Arrange sliced potatoes as for a scalloped dish, adding 1 T flour and salt and pepper between layers.

Arrange lean pork shops on top. Almost cover with milk. Pour ketchup over chops.

Cover and bake 350° for 1 hour. Remove cover and bake another 30 minutes to brown the top.

J.F.
Missouri

Delicious Dumplings

To 1 cup of chicken broth, add enough flour to roll out. Cut into squares and drop into broth. Cook until done or about 12 minutes. Very good, hot or cold.

Quick Dried Beef Dinner

Brown 1/2 lb. dried beef in 2 T butter.
Add 2 T flour, mix well.
Add 2 cups milk, bring to a boil.
Serve on rice, toast or corn bread.

Excellent Roast Beef

For a perfect roast beef either in a roaster in the oven or a pot roast on the cook stove, after braising, cook at very low heat no more than 250° with 1 cup water added. Cook for 3 or 4 hours.

Eggs and Cracklings

Heat 1/2 cup pork cracklings in a fry pan and scramble eggs into it. Use 1/2 cup for every two eggs.

I still love this dish and have our butcher coarse grind very fat pork. I slowly bake it till crisp, then drain the lard off before scrambling in the eggs. I keep the lard in a container in the refrigerator or freezer to have on hand for other uses.

Ann Kadlecek
Phillips, Wisconsin

Prime Rib

Prime rib wrapped in bacon and cooked in very slow oven is the secret to tender and juicy prime rib.

The *Learn-A-Lot Homemakers of Shawano, Wisconsin,* decided in the summer of 1996 to reenact cooking of the 1930's for their annual picnic. They chose the Great Depression as their theme, using only recipes from that period. It was an overwhelmingly successful gathering and they've shared some of their best recipes on the following pages.

159

Spinach Salad With Hot Bacon Dressing

4 slices bacon: fry crisp and take bacon out of pan

Mix: 1/2 c sugar
         1/2 t salt
         1/4 c vinegar
         1 c water
         1 T cornstarch
         1 beaten egg

Add to bacon grease; stir and cook over low heat until thickened. Pour hot over fresh spinach, 2 chopped green onions, and 2 chopped hard boiled eggs.

Depression Hot Dish

Fry crisp and drain 4 to 6 slices bacon.

Saute onions.

Add carrots and potatoes, sliced.

Season to taste.

Put into casserole and add one can cream style corn on top.

Bake 45 to 60 minutes.

Homemade Salad Dressing For Potato Salad

Put 1 c sugar, 1 c vinegar, and 1 c water in saucepan; bring to a boil.

In mixing bowl put 1 slightly heaping T flour, 1 T cornstarch, 1 t dry mustard, and 1 t salt. Moisten with water. Add 1 beaten egg.

Pour the hot liquid over ingredients in bowl. Stir well and pour all back into saucepan. Cook 2 or 3 minutes.

Pour into glass jar. When using, mix with a little sour cream.

Mix above with potatoes, onion, hard boiled eggs, parsley, celery (optional), salt and pepper to taste.

Jumble-La-La

1 lb hamburger
2 to 3 slices bacon (opt)
1/2 onion
1 c uncooked rice (not instant)
4 c tomatoes (whole, stewed, or juice)
1 t curry powder, to taste
2 or 3 bay leaves
1/4 to 1/2 c sugar (less if tomatoes are sweet)
4 c water
salt & pepper

Brown hamburger, bacon, onion, (can also add green pepper). Add rest of ingredients. Bake 2 hours at 350° (stir once or twice). May also be cooked on top of stove; stir in heavy saucepan until done.

Porcupine Meat Balls

1/3 c uncooked rice (not minute)
1 lb ground beef
1/2 t pepper
1 1/4 t salt
1 T minced onion
1/4 c canned tomato
1 t baking powder

Form into 12 meat balls. Place in greased casserole (don't brown). Pour additional 1 3/4 cup tomatoes over. (May use 1 can tomato soup and 1 small can tomato sauce, but the 30's version uses home-canned tomatoes.) Bake uncovered 35 minutes in 400° oven. Cover and bake 30 minutes longer, basting once or twice. (A pinch of marjoram was sometimes added.)

Old Time Baked Beans

Cook navy beans by adding cold water to 2 cups of washed beans to stand 1 inch above beans.

Bring to boil slowly and simmer several hours. Beans will be whole and tender. Don't add soda for quick cooking. Put in bean cooker or roaster.

Combine:

> 1/4 lb salt pork, bacon, or ham hocks
> (salt pork or bacon should be browned and
> drained)
> 2 1/2 cups water
> 1 t dry mustard
> 1 t salt
> 2 T brown sugar
> 2 T molasses
> 1 T vinegar
> 1/2 onion grated or cut up

Add above ingredients to beans and bake at 450° for 15 minutes covered. Uncover and bake at least 45 minutes longer. Beans should be brown but not dry. Water may be added if needed.

Garden Casserole

Slice 2 onions into a well-greased casserole.

Add 4 large sliced (thin) potatoes and 2 cups corn (fresh or frozen).

Add: 1 lb fried and drained pork sausage
      1 t salt
      1/4 t pepper

Pour 2 cups canned tomatoes over all. Top with buttered crumbs.

Bake covered 30 minutes. Remove cover and bake until golden brown and crusty.

Eggless, Milkless, Butterless Cake

2 c packed brown sugar
2 c water
4 T lard (or shortening)
2 c raisins
3 c flour
2 t baking soda
1 t salt
2 t cinnamon
1 t ground cloves

In pan combine sugar, water, lard, and raisins. Bring to boil; reduce heat and simmer 5 minutes. Cool. Combine dry ingredients and stir into cool raisin mixture. Mix well. Pour in greased 9 x 13 pan. Bake 350° for 45 minutes, or until it tests done. Yields 16 pieces.

———————————

Raspberry Bavarian Cream

1 pkg. raspberry jello
1 c boiling water
1/2 c sugar
1 c raspberry juice & water
1 c cream, whipped
2 c fresh raspberries, crushed & drained (or use frozen)

Dissolve jello in boiling water. Add sugar, raspberry juice and water. Chill. When slightly thickened, beat with rotary beater until fluffy. Fold in cream and berries. Chill.

———————————

Rhubarb Crunch

8 c rhubarb, diced
2 c sugar
4 T cornstarch
2 c water
2 t vanilla

Crumb Topping:
2 c flour
1 1/2 c rolled oats
2 c brown sugar
1 c butter
1 t cinnamon

In 4 qt. saucepan combine sugar, cornstarch, water and vanilla. Cook, stirring until thick and clear. Remove from heat. Stir in rhubarb. Mix together crumb topping until crumbly. Press half into 9 x 13 or larger pan. Pour rhubarb mixture over. Top with remaining crumbs. Bake at 350° for 1 hr. Cut in squares. Serve warm or cold, plain or topped with whipped cream.

———————————

MY FAMILY RECOLLECTIONS

Chapter 7

Give Us This Day
Our Daily Bread

GIVE US THIS DAY OUR DAILY BREAD

How fortunate for those of us during the Great Depression who could say our plea was answered.

Twila M. Will of Wausau, Wisconsin remembers the crusty "heel" cut off a fresh loaf of bread while still warm as being the best part, slathered with plenty of butter. Baking bread was a twice weekly event in her home as a child.

" Mother used a 'starter'. This was apparently a form of the now popular sour-dough. The starter was kept in a quart jar in the back of the flour bin of our Sellers kitchen cabinet, a dark, relatively cool place. In those Depression days, although we did have an ice-box, we couldn't afford ice.

When baking day came, the starter was taken out of hiding. It's contents, all but several spoonfuls, were emptied into a large crockery bowl. Cooled potato water was added. Then some sugar, a dollop of bacon grease or lard, and some flour. At that point the dough was about the consistency of cake batter, only more elastic. It was then set aside in a warm place to allow the yeast to multiply. When bubbles came to the top, it indicated that the starter was alive. Several spoonfuls were placed into the starter jar and it was returned to its hiding place in the flour bin. The rest was mixed with more flour until it achieved the denseness of bread dough. After thoroughly kneading it, it was covered and set aside in a warm place to rise. As the dough lifted the lid, it was punched down, kneaded again and allowed to rise. After the second rising, it was again kneaded and formed into loaves. These were allowed to rise and then were baked in the oven.

In the winter, the coal fired kitchen range did the honors. In the summer, the oil-stove oven was used so the kitchen did not get so hot.

If Mother was in a good mood, she might allow us to cut the heels off one loaf, smear them with butter, and enjoy them as an afternoon snack. Heaven!!

Twila M. Will
Wausau, Wisconsin

This starter was also called "Herman Starter". It was rejuvenated by adding warm potato water and sugar and allowed to rest in a dark warm place until the next baking which usually was in several days.

Crusty White Bread

Dissolve 2 pkg. yeast in 2 cups warm water until frothy.

Stir in 1/2 c sugar, 2 t salt, 2 beaten eggs, 1/4 c melted margarine or butter.

Mix well and add 3 cups white flour.

Beat vigorously and add 3 more cups flour, mix and knead to satiny smoothness. Knead 10 minutes using another 1/2 c flour as needed.

Place into greased bowl, cover with towel and allow to rise until double.

Punch down well. Form into two loaves and place in well greased pans. Bake 375° for 35 to 40 minutes.

Whole Wheat Bread

Combine and stir well:
2 t salt
4 T brown sugar
4 T molasses
2 T melted shortening
2 c hot water

Blend:
1 pkg. dry yeast
3/4 c dry milk

Add to warm mixture above along with 3 c flour. Beat with mixer till smooth.
Add 1 c more of white flour, beat well.
Add 2 c whole wheat flour. Knead for a few minutes. Rise. Punch down. Rise again and shape into two loaves, greasing pans well. Rise to double. Bake 350° 45 to 55 minutes or until nicely browned.

Maple Wheat Bread

Take out of refrigerator and place on counter to bring to room temperature 2 eggs, maple syrup and margarine.

Put 1 1/4 c water into sauce pan. Add 3/4 c maple syrup and 1/3 c margarine.

Bring to warm temperature or till margarine is melted. Pour into large mixing bowl and cool to luke warm.

Mix in 2 pkg. dry yeast, let set for two minutes.

Add 1 t salt, 1 t cinnamon, 1/2 t nutmeg, 2 well beaten eggs, 1 c raisins (optional).

Mix till well blended. Add 2 1/2 c all purpose flour, mixing well.

Finish with 2 to 3 cups whole wheat flour or enough to make a satiny smooth dough. Grease well and rise to double in size.

Knead again and form into two loaves. Grease pans well.

Bake 375° for 30 minutes. Brush tops with butter when cooling.

Joyce Stanley
Minnetonka, Minnesota

Rachel's Oatmeal Bread

1 cake yeast
1/4 c water
1 t sugar
1/4 c shortening
1 T salt
1/4 c brown sugar
1/3 c molasses
1 c oatmeal
1 c boiling water
1 c cold water
5 1/2 c flour

Put yeast in warm water annd let rise.

Mix shortening, salt, boiling water, brown sugar, oatmeal, molasses. Stir well.

Add cold water and yeast.

Add flour gradually. Knead.

Raise 2 hours or so. Shape into 2 loaves. Rise 1 hour.

Bake 425° for 15 minutes, then 350° for 30 - 45 minutes.

When bottom of pan sizzles when touched with wet finger, it's done.

From the collection of
Rachel Schermer Paske

Rich Yeast Dough

For Christmas kuchen or holiday breads or rolls.

In large mixing bowl combine 2 cups flour and 1 pkg. dry yeast.

Heat 1 c milk, 1/2 c butter, 1/4 c sugar, 1 t salt until butter is melted.

Cool to luke warm and add to dry mixture. Add 1 beaten egg.

Beat well with mixer and add 1/1/2 c more flour to make a soft dough.

Knead for 5 minutes well.

Turn into greased bowl, turn once to grease all sides and allow to rise until double. Makes two loaves or 24 rolls.

For Holiday Kuchen add after first mixing 1 c mixed candied fruit, 1 c raisins, 3/4 c nuts. Form into flat loaves and bake 20 to 25 minutes in 350° oven.

Cool on racks and ice with powdered sugar icing.

TASTY BREAD TOPPING

A by-product of butchering, pork cracklings were plentiful and women found a variety of ways to use them, as in scrambled eggs, cookies, etc.

Alvina Alm of Sauk Center, Minnesota made an exceptionally delicious topping she served her family on fresh baked bread. Easy to make, you simply grind cracklings and add cooked apples to make a spreading consistency.

Dorothy Van Amber
Alexandria, Minnesota

BEDTIME SNACKS

"Everything was either scarce or priced beyond our means during the Great Depression, especially for people on small farms. What was plentiful though was milk, bread, potatoes and garden vegetables, fresh in the summer and canned in winter.

One of my snack foods in those days was home baked white bread broken up in a glass of milk. We called it simply 'bread and milk'. It was my favorite, but when I told my children about this simple treat they were revolted by such crude fare."

Walter L. Radley
Oshkosh, Wisconsin

BISCUIT KNOW HOW

"You had to know how to make good use of everything. Large batches of biscuits were made every morning on a daily basis. They were good. Pure lard gave them the flavor and kept them fresh for awhile. Often it solved more than just the food problem and there were always old biscuits around. When you were ready to leave the house and you noticed your shoes needed buffing, a part of the biscuit did that job quite nicely. Banana peels worked too, but who ever had a banana."

Lessons from Grandma Lillian Sparks
Mary Paske
Maryville, Tennessee

Extra Light Biscuits

Mix together 1 c milk with 1/2 teaspoon soda.

Mix 2 cups flour with 3/4 teaspoon salt, 1 tablespoon sugar, 2 teaspoons baking powder.

Add to milk and soda along with 2 tablespoons melted shortening.

Knead lightly. Roll out to 1/2 inch thickness. Brush top with shortening and fold over.

Cut out and bake in 450° degree preheated oven for 12 to 15 minutes, or till nicely browned. Buttermilk can also be used.

Buttermilk Biscuits

Set oven at 450°.

Sift 1 3/4 cups flour with 1 teaspoon salt, 2 teaspoons baking powder, 1 teaspoon sugar and 1/2 teaspoon soda.

Cut in 1/4 c butter and finish with finger tips until mixture resembles crumbs.

Add anywhere from 2/3 to 3/4 c buttermilk, enough to make a soft dough but not sticky.

On floured board knead until smooth.

Roll out and cut into squares or cut with cooky cutter.

Bake 10 to 12 minutes or until brown.

Sausage Gravy

Fry till crisp 1/2 lb. pork sausage, using a heavy fry pan. Remove sausage and stir in 1/3 c flour stirring to cook through but not to brown. Add 2 cups cold milk, gradually stirring all the while. Bring to a boil. Season with lots of pepper, add sausage. Serve over fresh biscuits.

Muffins

When I can applesauce I leave the apples in chunks. Then I make apple muffins as in Volume I, page 141. I use the canned apples instead of fresh. I drain them and use the juice instead of milk in the muffin batter. If it's a little too dry I add milk and bake 30 to 35 minutes. It's very good. I have done Depression cooking all my life.

Carl J. Holland
Berlin, Wisconsin

Sourdough Bread Starter

Mix together 2 c warm water with 1 pkg. dry yeast and 2 cups flour.

Put into a 2 qt. bowl and allow to set 48 hours at room temperature.

Stir two or three times. After 48 hours cover tightly and refrigerate.

To use stir and pour off required amount.

To the rest add 1 c warm water and 1 c flour mixing very well. Let stand for 5 or 6 hours at room temperature or until it bubbles. Then refrigerate again.

Sourdough Bread

Mix well (or use blender for this) 1 c warm water, 1 pkg dry yeast, 2 T sugar and 2 t salt. Add 1 1/2 c sour dough starter and mix very well. Scrape sides of bowl often.

Add 1 1/2 c flour, beating well.

When batter is nice and smooth add 1 1/2 c flour and beat well again, scraping sides to make a smooth batter.

Add 1 more c flour and mix till smooth. Cover bowl and allow to rise till double in size, about 1 1/2 hours.

Turn out on floured board, work in 1 more c of flour, approx. Knead 5 minutes or more. Shape into 2 loaves. Rise another 1 1/2 hours.

Bake 40 minutes in 400° oven using a shallow pan of water on rack below the loaf pans. Crust will be dark brown when finished baking.

Kathy's Popovers

Turn oven on 450°. Grease 12 muffin tins.

Beat 4 eggs slightly. Add 2 c milk, 1 t salt, 2 T oil, and 2 c flour.

Beat till almost smooth. *DO NOT OVERBEAT!*

Fill pans 1/2 full, bake 25 minutes at 450°. *DO NOT OPEN OVEN DOOR!*

Lower temperature to 300° and bake another 25 minutes or until nicely browned.

Serve hot with butter and jam.

_____

Mankind has long depended on bread for subsistence. All varieties, from the early unleavened Biblical breads to todays multitude of choices. All satisfy the pallet and have been the mainstay of meals and lunches for all time. There has been and is available every type of bread one could wish for.

One variety which came with the pioneers is the "filled breads" which took the place of a meal. They were popular in hard times because the ingredients for the fillings were from the vegetable gardens or from cheeses and eggs, all of which were easily available. They were originally prepared for hearty lunches for outdoor workers, as pasties were.

A delicious and hearty sauerkraut bread is favored today for outings and suppers. The recipe originally came from the Ukraine but has also been prepared in some form in many other countries. The following bread recipe was especially popular in the 1930's because it used honey in place of sugar and sometimes no shortening as in the recipe that follows.

_____

Sauerkraut Bread

Frozen sweet roll dough may also be used. The original calls for: 1 1/2 cups warm water
1 yeast cake
1/2 c honey

Beat all together vigorously, set aside till it bubbles.

Add 3 cups whole wheat flour and 2 t salt. Beat well.

Finish with enough white flour to make a soft dough. Knead 10 minutes.

Rise till double in size. Punch down and divide in half, making two rectangles.

Place one into greased 9 x 13 size pan.

Prepare filling while bread is rising. Spread on dough to very edges.

Filling:
Drain 2 cups sauerkraut till almost dry.

Add 1 shredded carrot, 2 bay leaves, 1 T sugar and simmer until quite dry.

Remove bay leaf. Spoon onto dough and spread evenly.

Cover with remaining rectangle of dough. Pinch edges shut. Brush with egg white, make several slits on top. Rise till double.

Bake 350° for 45 minutes or until nicely browned.

Feta Bread

Using sweet dough (recipe above) arrange rectangle as above in greased 9 x 13 pan.

Crumble 1/2 c Feta cheese over and break 3 large eggs into it. Do not break yolks. Pour 1 beaten egg over this.

Cover with remaining rectangle of dough.

Pinch shut, brush with egg white, cut several slits.

Set aside to rise till double.

Bake at 350 degrees till nicely browned, about 45 minutes.

Mil's Kraut Kuchen

Millie grew up on this recipe, and her own family still begs for it today. A nice soft roll dough is rolled out after the first rise, cut into squares and filled with the following delicious filling. Brown hamburger, add sliced cabbage and onion, and saute' a bit to cook through. Add filling to each square, then fold diagonally to make a triangle, pinching the two sides shut. Rise again, bake like rolls and serve warm.

Mil Levenhagen
Neenah, Wisconsin

CANADIAN BAKIN'
(Chicago 1933)

I learned to love a mystery during the Great Depression when I was four-going-on-five. Grandma was the main source of mystification in my life. She could read the future in tea leaves, but couldn't find her spectacles or her reticule (purse). She spoke a foreign language (Canadian) so that her words for things were not the words my modern American mother had taught me. Grandma's frequent use of what I thought were Canadian words: "Whatcha-may-call-it" and "What's-her-name" also added to the puzzle of her intended meaning. Unable to resist the challenge of conversing with Grandma, however, I searched her out one morning and found her in the kitchen contemplating two white hills on her baking board. I poked an exploratory finger into one.

"Go wash your hands."
"They're clean, Grandma."
"Not clean enough to stick in my biscuit dough."

I am confused. I haven't touched any dough. I have merely made a slight dent in one of the hills.

"Grandma, are you going to have trees?"
Now Grandma looks puzzled, "What do you mean—trees?"
"On your hills. Are you going to have trees?"
"They are not hills. They are heaps. Now go wash your hands like I told you."

When I return I find that Grandma has assembled salt, baking powder, lard and milk. I deduct correctly that the hills must be flour and Grandma is baking.

185

"Sit there, watch me, and don't touch" warns Grandma.
"But Grandma, I washed my... "
"Sit, watch and listen. Do you know what a receipt is?"
"Yes, you get one when you pay."
"This is different. It tells you what to use when you want to make something."

So far, so good. The Canadian word for "recipe" must be "receipt."

"My receipt calls for two heaps of flour."
"Where is it?"
"Right in front of you. What you called hills are heaps."
"No, I mean where is the receipt?"
"In my head."

I look at Grandma's soft gray hair piled in curls on top of her head. I even check one ear. No sign of a recipe. Learning to cook in a foreign language is going to be a bigger challenge for a "four-going-on-five-year-old" than I expected. I watch Grandma sift the flour along with a big handful of baking powder and a little one of salt. After she has sifted three times she uses her largest serving spoon to scoop out two mounds of lard. These she blends into the flour mixture with two knives. She hands me the spoon.

"Now make a well in the whatcha-may-call-it, and pour in the milk."

I figure "well" must be the Canadian word for "hole," because Grandma does not object to the hole I have made. She lets me pour in a large mug of milk. The second mug she pours in gradually stirring all the time. While Grandma checks the oven I get to smear lard all over two cookie sheets. This is fun.

Grandma drops the dough into heaps on the cookie sheets and places them in the oven. Fifteen minutes later we have hot buttered biscuits with tea. Yum!

Note: Because Grandma used the slower acting baking powder, and not many people cook by heaps, mounds, handsful and pinches I have translated Grandma's Canadian Drop Biscuit Receipt into American below. The biscuits were good with any meal of the day, and a special breakfast treat was "Canadian" bacon, eggs and drop biscuits. The biscuits were also halved horizontally, smothered in fresh strawberries and topped with whipped cream for Sunday dinner dessert. Delicious!

This is approximately half of **Grandma's Drop Biscuit** recipe:

2 c flour
1 T baking powder
1/2 t salt
1/3+ c lard (1/3 rounded)
1 c plus 1 ounce milk

Sift flour, baking powder and salt. Cut in lard with a pastry blender. Add milk stirring only until well mixed. Drop by rounded tablespoons onto well greased cookie sheet. Bake in oven that has been preheated to 450 ° for 15 minutes or until brown. Serve hot. This recipe makes 10 to 12 biscuits. To reheat biscuits sprinkle with water and heat uncovered, but touching at 425° until hot, 10-12 minutes. (Grandma put them in her cast iron Dutch oven for reheating.)

Later I discovered that Grandma's expressions were not particularly Canadian but rather old-fashioned. Her nouns she had lost in a stroke, thus the frequent use of "Whatcha-may-call-it" and "What's-her-name." I suspect that Grandma got this particular recipe from "What's-her-name."

Edith Peterson
Wausau, Wisconsin

CHILDREN WORRIED TOO

In this house father didn't charge a dimes worth, no matter what the need. You didn't go around making bills you didn't know how to pay. Besides, you couldn't embarrass yourself that way. You didn't charge or borrow. You might swap for something, but you always made it right. Father also did all of the buying right down to the last grocery item.

Dolores remembers the day as a small girl when father was down in bed with the flu and mother noticed the big barrel of flour was almost empty. The double catastrophe of father being sick in bed and not having flour in the house was too much for a little girl and Dolores went off crying with a real fear of the future.

Dolores Markstrum
Wausau, Wisconsin

It was a horrible time. I remember Mom saying, "we have no more flour for bread". We were nine children and I was the oldest. I said to Mom, we'll have to pray, which we all proceeded to do. In a few minutes we got a call from the dime store asking me to come to work for that day. I worked all day long and was paid 97 cents. I went directly to the grocery store and asked how much a 25 pound sack of flour would cost. The man said 97 cents. Our prayer was answered. God is so good.

Vera Peterson
Sheboygan, Michigan

ELDERBERRY FLOWER PANCAKES

Oh, those wonderful cakes. Carl Holland from Berlin, Wisconsin can still see his mom picking up Elderberry flowers by the stem and putting them on the pancakes upside down. Then she turned them pulling the stems off, leaving the flowers in the cakes. How can anyone ever forget that.

The pancake batter might have been the tried and true favorite recipe used in almost every household.

Delicious Buttermilk Cakes

Mix 1 c flour with 1 T sugar, 1/2 t salt and 1/2 t soda.
Add 1 egg, 2 T melted shortening and 1 c buttermilk.
Fry on a medium hot griddle.

Or some families made the original ''Awesome Blossom''. The batter was thinned just a trifle, blossoms with stems left on were dipped in the batter and deep fried in a pan of hot lard. Sometimes they were dusted with powdered or plain sugar, but generally were served as is. The largest serving platter was used to bring them to the table. Leftovers were unheard of.

Children would become tired of the same oatmeal or cornmeal mush for breakfast, year in and out. *Ralph Trudeau*'s mother had an answer for that. She combined them and made a new breakfast cereal dish.

To 1 part old fashioned oatmeal add the same amount of corn meal. Use 2 cups water and dash of salt for 1 c cereal. Cook until nice and creamy. Save leftovers in greased bread pans. When cool fry in lard for another meal.

190

Molasses Cake

1 c brown or white sugar
1/2 c lard
1 egg
3/4 c molasses
1 t baking powder
1 t cinnamon
1/4 t cloves
1/2 t nutmeg
1/2 t salt
2 c flour
1 t soda
1 c sour milk

Cream shortening and sugar. Add egg. Sift together the baking powder, salt, spices and flour. Add baking soda to sour milk. Add molasses to sugar, lard and egg mixture. Add dry ingredients alternately with sour milk and soda. Bake in 9 x 13 pan at 350° for 30 minutes or until toothpick inserted in cake comes out clean.

———————————

Johnny Cake

1 c cornmeal
1 c flour
1/4 c sugar
1/2 t salt
2 t baking powder

1 c milk
1 egg, beaten
4 T melted lard or shortening

Heat oven to 400°. Grease 8 or 9 inch pan. Combine dry ingredients. Stir in milk, egg and melted shortening, mixing until dry ingredients are moistened. Pour batter into prepared pan. Bake 20 to 25 minutes, or until golden brown and toothpick inserted near center comes out clean. Serve warm. 9 servings.

Corn Krispies

Preheat oven to 425°.

Mix 1 c cornmeal, 1 c boiling water, 3/4 t salt and 2 T shortening.

Ladle onto buttered cookie sheet and smooth out to cover bottom of pan.

Bake until delicately browned. Cut with pizza cutter into strips or squares.

Cool. Can also be made into cooky shapes. They're great for snacks.

A. Olson
Scranton, Pennsylvania

50 Minute Hot Cross Buns

Dissolve 1 pkg dry yeast in 1/4 c warm water.

Beat 1 egg. Add 1 c warm water, 1/3 c melted butter, 3/4 t salt, 1/4 c sugar.

Mix well and add yeast.

Add 3 c flour to which has been added 1 t cinnamon, 1 c raisins, 1/4 c citron.

Knead and allow to rise till double.

Form into buns, rise, bake at 350° for 20 minutes or until nicely golden brown.

When cool frost a cross on top of each with icing made of 2 T milk, 1/2 t vanilla, and 1/2 c powdered sugar.

YOU HAD TO SELL THE EGGS

"When I was a young girl, still living with my parents, I was asked by a neighbor to help her with her work in her home during an illness. This neighbor and her husband lived on a large farm and among the many things I needed to do during the time I spent there was to make the meals. Especially interesting to me was a recipe for scrambled eggs I was sure to use most of the time for breakfast. Because eggs were a precious commodity that needed to be sold for cash to buy groceries, the ones we used for ourselves had to go a long way. Here was a way to stretch a few eggs into a big bowl of scrambled eggs.

Since the Depression lasted into the early years of my homemaking I often used this recipe for my own family and they never tired of it. It was a way to get a lot of mileage out of a few eggs.

Scrambled Eggs

Beat 2 or 3 eggs and add 2 cups milk.
Mix 3 cups flour, 1 teaspoon baking powder and 1 teaspoon salt.
Sift into eggs and milk mixture and beat until smooth.
Have ready 1/4 c lard hot in a skillet.
Add batter and turn to medium high.
Use a knife to lift dough as it browns adding more lard if needed.
Keep stirring with knife and when all batter is about baked, break into marble size with spatula and keep browning. Serve with syrup or sugar.

Ruth Bohm
Wausau, Wisconsin

Norwegian Pancakes

Another popular standby was the ethnic oven-baked pancakes. The following recipe was made in a glass pie plate, but often was doubled and baked in a large cake loaf pan.

Preheat oven to 425°.

Melt 3 T butter in the pan.

Meanwhile mix 1/2 c flour, 1/2 c milk and 2 eggs.

Add a 1/2 t cardamom or nutmeg and pour into sizzling pan.

Bake for 15 to 20 minutes or until nicely browned.

Serve with jelly, jam or syrup. (Original recipe calls for mulberry, gooseberry or elderberry jam.)

Emily Svenson
St. Paul, Minnesota

The Dutch also relied heavily on this recipe for delicious filling breakfasts. Their version is very similar.

Dutch Pancakes

Preheat oven to 400°. Beat 3 eggs.

Add 3/4 c milk and 3/4 c flour mixed with 1 t sugar, 1 t nutmeg and a dash of salt.

Pour into a hot 9 x 13 pan sizzling in 2 T butter.

Bake 15 to 20 minutes and serve at once with jams or syrups.

Or dust with powdered sugar and drizzle with lemon wedges.

MY FAMILY RECOLLECTIONS

Chapter 8

Goodies of the Day

IT WAS " WE & OURS"

Couples were very close. When you married that special man or that sweet young girl you knew it was for life. You also expected to take the good with the bad, the bitter with the sweet. Every experience shared together strengthened that bond until you read each other like a book and you counted on each other 100%. You arrived at the same decisions after a while, and while you slept, you occasionally dreamed the same dreams. You were forever two together facing the world and holding your own very well. It was a comfortable way to go through life. You were well taken care of.

Everything you owned belonged to both equally. It was automatic and understood. And thus it was that the Cartwrights of Elk Mound, Wisconsin, shared "our recipe" for a Never Fail Meringue. Used through a life time of great cooking, it will make any cook proud.

"For this cause a man shall leave his father and mother, and shall cleave to his wife; and the two shall become one flesh."

The Book of Genesis

Never Fail Meringue

Dissolve 1 T Cornstarch in 1 1/2 T cold water.

Add to 1/2 cup boiling water in sauce pan. Cook till clear and set aside to cool with cover on.

Beat from 3 to 5 egg whites until they stand in soft peaks.

Beat in cooled paste. Continue beating until firm peaks form.

Beat in 6 T. sugar one at a time while continuing to beat until nice and firm but not dry. Add 1/2 t vanilla.

Spoon meringue all the way to edge of pie crust. Bake in 400° oven till nicely browned.

Marv & Charlotte Cartwright

MOTHER'S PIE CRUST RECIPE

When I was newly married I asked my Mother how to make good pie crust like she made. She said, "Use lard, of course, and a couple handfuls of flour, a pinch or two of salt, and enough water to hold it together. Then you work it until it feels right." I asked, "But if you never worked it how will you know?" Her answer was that I would know. After several tries I found the feel.

Betty Hainsworth
El Dorado Hills, California

"The Rumford Complete Cook Book" of 1935 suggests using less lard in pie crust to save money, and the addition of their Rumford Baking Powder helps create a "light, flaky and tender (crust) without being too rich." Their recipe follows.

Short Paste

3 c flour
1 t salt
1 t Rumford Baking Powder
1 c lard, or other shortening
Ice-cold water to mix

Sift together the flour, salt and baking powder; work in the shortening lightly with the fingers, mix to a firm dough with the ice-cold water and roll out once on a floured board. Use for whatever purpose desired.

For even less fat, they suggest using 1 1/2 c flour, 1 t baking powder, and 1/2 c lard or shortening. This would be even more agreeable for today's health-conscious cooks.

———————————

Grandma's Rhubarb Custard Pie

Use a deep dish pie pan and one unbaked bottom crust.

Prepare 2 c cut up rhubarb. Put half into unbaked crust.

Mix 1 3/4 c sugar, 3 T flour, dash of salt, 1/2 t vanilla and 1/2 t cinnamon.

Beat 3 eggs and mix with above.

Pour half over rhubarb. Cover with whole graham crackers.

Add rest of rhubarb and top this with the rest of the egg mixture.

Sprinkle cinnamon on top.

Bake 350° until knife comes out clean, about 45 minutes. Cover edge of crust with foil to prevent overbaking.

Sour Cream Raisin Pie

This is an original recipe dating back over 100 years, still enjoyed today in the home of Dorothy Westerberg of Prescott, Wisconsin. The recipe comes from her 93 year young Mother who has served it throughout most of her lifetime.

1 c sour cream (lite or regular)
1/2 c seeded raisins, finely ground
1/2 t cinnamon
1/4 t cloves

pinch of salt
1/2 c sugar
3 egg yolks, beaten

Mix the above and cook until thick. Pour into an 8 in. baked pie shell.
Prepare meringue with the 3 egg whites, filling crust to very edges.
Bake 400° until slightly browned.

Tillie Bergman
Prescott, Wisconsin

RAISIN PIES

You always had raisin pie for the fellows. You would send it out to lunch for the hard working field workers or threshing crew or pack it for bag lunches. It was cut into pieces and enjoyed from the hand. With a pot of coffee and a sandwich or two it was very satisfying and stayed with the men for hours of more work.

Charlotte Cartwright of Elk Mound, Wisconsin has made raisin pie for her husband from the time they were married 50 some years ago.

Her mother-in-law gave her the recipe and also taught her how to serve this pie. It was brought to the table cut into serving size pieces. A fork was not provided because the pie was eaten from the hand like a cookie.

203

Charlotte's Raisin Pie

Pour 1 c hot water over 1 c raisins.

Mix 3/4 c sugar with 2 T flour or cornstarch.

Beat well 1 egg, add to raisins and cook until thick.

Pour into an 8 inch unbaked pie shell. Add top crust, sprinkle with sugar.

Bake 425° oven for 30 to 40 minutes.

Marvin & Charlotte Cartwright
Elk Mound, Wisconsin

Gracie's Blue Ribbon Lemon Pie

Moisten 7 rounded T cornstarch with water.

Add 1 1/2 c sugar, 2 c water, 1/4 t salt, and 1 1/2 T butter. Cook until thickened, about 10 minutes.

Add juice and rind of two lemons (or 1/2 c). Bring to a boil.

Mix 5 egg yolks with 2 T milk, mixing well.

Stir hot mixture gently into egg yolks. Bring to a boil again, then cool.

Fill baked, cooled pie shell and cover with meringue all the way to edges.

Meringue:
Beat 5 egg whites till good and frothy.

Add 1/2 c sugar mixed with 1 1/2 T cornstarch, 1 T at a time. Beat till stiff peaks form.

Bake 400° 10 minutes or until nice and deep golden.

From the collection of
Grace Rivas
Cornell, Wisconsin

Favorite Pumpkin Pie

Prepare one unbaked pie shell.

Combine 1/2 c sugar, 1/4 t ginger, 1/2 t cinnamon, 1/2 t salt.

Add 2 slightly beaten eggs, 1 c pumpkin, 1 c milk, and 1 t vanilla.

Pour into crust and bake 15 minutes at 450°.

Reduce heat to 350° and bake till knife comes out clean, about 45 minutes in all.

On the farm in central Mississippi where I grew up during and after the depression, we raised almost all our food. During the summer we canned, pickled, preserved, jellied and dried foods to sustain us through the winter. One of my favorite winter treats was fried pies, made from apples we had dried the previous summer. When the apples were harvested we peeled them, sliced them thinly and laid them out on sheets of corrugated tin in the hot sun to dry. Those apples were soaked overnight before cooking, but processing of apples now makes that step unnecessary.

Fried Apple Pies

Pastry:
2 1/2 c flour
1/2 t salt
3/4 c lard
1/2 c cold water

Combine flour and salt, cut lard into mixture. Add cold water, adding more if necessary until pastry holds together. Chill.

Filling:
6 ounces dried apples
2 1/4 c water
1/2 c sugar
1 t cinnamon
1/8 t nutmeg
1 T butter

Cook apples in 2 c of water, adding more if necessary, about 30 minutes, or until apples are tender and begin to fall apart. Add sugar, cinnamon, nutmeg and butter. While apples are still warm, make pies as follows: Form dough into balls about the size of a small egg. Roll each into a circle, place a tablespoonful of apple mixture on one half of the dough. Fold the other half over the apples, crimp edges closed with tines of a fork. In a large cast iron skillet heat about 1/2 inch of lard to medium-hot. Fry a couple of pies at a time, about 2-3 minutes on each side, until brown. Sprinkle with sugar if desired.

Doris Dolph
Schofield, Wisconsin

We called them "Nothings"

If you were short of everything in the pantry you almost always still could make this nutritious snack for lunch or when company might drive up.

Heat fat for deep frying. Slightly beat up as many eggs as you think you'll need for this lunch. Add a pinch of salt and enough flour to make a soft dough. Roll very thin. Cut into squares or diamonds. Cut a slit into the center and pull the point through and back again. Fry in hot fat. Dust with powdered sugar or plain sugar.

LaCrosse, Wisconsin

SUMMER KITCHENS

Cherished childhood memories linger lifelong and Janet Knutson of Gully, Minnesota takes us back to the popular summer kitchens many homes enjoyed before air conditioning became a fact of life.

"My Aunt Emily's summer kitchen... what a wonderful place for a child to explore. Aunt Emily's summer kitchen was furnished with items some would cast away, yet they were good enough for this kitchen. The old black stove with the reservoir full of warm water to do the dishes, and the round oak table covered by the flowered oil cloth and surrounded by assorted chairs and stools. The walls were bare wood with the 2 x 4's exposed. Behind the table Uncle Albert nailed boards between the 2x4's to make shelves and extra seating. The sink was a great find.. porcelain, with a drainboard big enough to wash milk pails, and a bucket underneath to catch the used water. Everywhere there were great big kettles and enormous bowls for cooking large amounts of food to feed threshing or haying crews, or the like. It had lots of windows with screens. The woodshed was right behind with stacks of dry wood for the cook stove.

Huge elm trees shaded the little house and the pathway to the big, incredibly neat house. When we would go to visit, the summer kitchen is where we would congregate. There, you didn't have to wipe your feet, and kids could sit and eat all kinds of wonderful goodies.

I especially remember boiled raisin cupcakes with brown sugar frosting, potato lefse, baked on the old wood stove, and sugar cookies... oh, so good! We had great pans of fried chicken and potato salad, watermelon, fresh buns by the dozen, spread lavishly with butter we helped churn in a big glass jar with wooden paddles turned by a crank. We had chokecherry jelly and plums to eat fresh.

We could help pick eggs and put the chickens in the hen house for the night; get the old jersey cow, then spray the flies off her back before milking.

I remember the old reel lawn mower that Albert kept sharp and well oiled. It was fun to make the grass fly behind it and form little hay stacks out of the grass.

Emily let me pick flowers and put them in vases and glass jars, mostly zinnias, snapdragons and marigolds. The hollyhocks grew tall along the house and morning glorys climbed the walls on strings. Their was goldenglo, little white button flowers, and the sweet peas, how I loved them. Golden memories in my treasure chest... how rich I am."

Janet Knutson
Gully, Minnesota

Janet's recipe for boiled raisin cupcakes:

Boiled Raisin Cupcakes

Cream together 1 c sugar with 1/4 c butter.

Add 2 beaten eggs.

Sift 2 1/2 c flour with 1 t soda, 1/4 t baking powder and 1/2 t each nutmeg, cinnamon, allspice and cloves.

Boil 2 c raisins in 1 c water. Cool.

Add to creamed mixture alternately with flour.

Bake 350° until done. Frost with brown sugar frosting.

Brown Sugar Frosting

1 1/2 c brown sugar
1/2 c white sugar
2/3 c cream

Boil till it forms a soft ball. Take off stove and cool. Then stir until creamy. Spread on cupcakes.

LOW FAT WAS IN

But not for the same reasons we do it today. In some homes butter was limited or non-existent. Homemakers always found a way to deal with shortages. They made up their own recipes and some frugal ones were handed down.

The Danes had a special thing about their delicious spicy Christmas cookies. Guests had to have one or it was believed they'd carry the Christmas spirit away. Recipes varied according to the families preference of spices, but the basic recipe remained for the most part the same. Huge cooky jars were used for the finished product. Often it was an earthen jar with a heavy plate on top to store and age the delicious, fragrant confections. Several recipes used through generations follow. The first is a good little cooky one took a handful of as you left the house. They carried well in a pocket and you always had your lunch with you.

Pebernodder

Or "Peppernuts", as they were called.

Boil 1 c corn syrup, 1/2 c sugar and 1/4 c butter. Cool. Sift in 3 1/2 c flour, 1 t each cloves and cinnamon, and pinch of soda. Grate in rind of 1 lemon. Knead the dough. Allow to stand in a warm place for two days. Knead dough again and roll out to 1/2 inch thickness. Cut into small pieces and roll each into a ball. Place on greased cooky sheets and bake at 350° for only 6 or 7 minutes or until golden. Makes 400 small cookies.

PEPPERNUTS

These gently spiced, crisp little cookies were enjoyed by Bob and Eleanor Eggebrecht of Wausau, Wisconsin even before they knew each other, and they've been married 57 years.

Both of their parents made them. Bob's grandparents had a large family of ten children and they all liked them so much that his grandmother made them in big batches and stored them in 50 pound flour sacks.

Their recipe is believed to have come from Germany with the Eggebrecht's ancestors. The popularity of Peppernuts in their family dates back to the 1800's and is still enjoyed by family members today, five generations later. The grandchildren love them and eat them by the handfuls.

Eggebrecht's Peppernuts

1 1/2 c lard or margarine
1 1/4 c brown sugar
1/2 c molasses
1 c dark corn syrup

Bring all to a boil until dissolved. Cool to room temperature.

Mix 1 1/4 t baking soda into 1/4 c sour milk or buttermilk. Add to above mixture.

Measure and sift the following spices in 1 c flour:
1/2 t each nutmeg, cloves, ginger, allspice
1/4 t each cardamom and anise
Dash of salt

Sift and add to mixture.

Add 1/2 t oil of anise (or to taste).

Add 6 to 8 c flour, or enough to make a stiff dough. The cookies will be flat if not enough flour is worked in.

Chill the dough.

When ready to bake, take a handful and roll with palms on counter into finger size or about 3/4 inch diameter. Cut into 1/2 inch slices. Place rounded side up, 1/2 inch apart on cooky sheet. (If you lay the cut dough flat on the cooky sheet, the cookies will be rounded like other cookies. By placing them vertically with rounded side up they bake into a unique pillow shape different from all other cookies.)

Bake about 10 minutes at 350° until a bit more brown on the bottom. If not done enough they may be flat after baking.

Cool on counter and store.

Submitted by
Roy Gullings
Wausau, Wisconsin

1934 Raisin Cookies

Ruth Giffen of Aledo, Illinois is still making the delicious raisin cookies she has been making since 1934. She never tires of this tried and true recipe which provided many a syrup bucket lunch treat for school kids of that time. Easy to prepare, it's a typical cooky of the Great Depression era. Free commodities given to people to help them through troubled times most often contained a large package of dried raisins along with other basic food items.

Cream 1/3 c shortening (Crisco is Ruth's favorite today) with 1 c sugar.

Soak and add 1/2 c raisins, 1/2 t vanilla and 1/8 t almond extract.

Combine 1 1/2 c flour with 1 t baking powder and 1/2 t salt.

Add the flour mixture alternately with 1/3 c milk.

Bake 10 minutes.

Ruth Giffen
Aledo, Illinois

———————————

Grandma Giovanna's Oatmeal Cookies

"This 'recipe' was given to me orally by Grandma Giovanna over 60 years ago. She did not have a written recipe, and neither have I since. Through the years this was my husband's favorite cookie."

Mix 1 c sugar with 1 large basting spoon lard or butter.

Add 2 eggs and mix well.

Mix in 1/2 c buttermilk (sweet milk will work).

Add 1/2 c flour sifted with 1 t soda, pinch of salt, 1 t cinnamon and 1/8 t nutmeg.

Add 2 c oatmeal, handful of raisins and 1/2 c walnut pieces, if on hand.

Drop by spoonfuls on greased cookie sheet.

Bake 350° until golden brown, 8 to 10 minutes.

Belvina Bertino
Osburn, Idaho

Very Good Chocolate Cake by Mom

Cream together 1 c sugar and 2 T Crisco.

Add 1 egg and beat some more.

Sift together 1 1/2 c flour with 8 T cocoa.

Add above mixture along with 1 c buttermilk to which 1 t soda has been added.

Add vanilla and beat well.

Bake 350° until cake tests done with toothpick.

(If you use chocolate in place of cocoa, use 2 squares and only 1 T Crisco.)

Never Fail Fudge Frosting

Bring to a full rolling boil:
1 c sugar
1/4 c milk
1/4 c butter
2 squares chocolate

Remove from heat. Add vanilla. Stir till spreading consistency.

Dorothy's Fudge Icing

Another simple to prepare but delicious icing used to satisfy a family of fudge cake lovers deserves to be passed on.

Melt 1/2 c butter in 1/4 c water.

Add 1/2 c cocoa, 2 1/2 c powdered sugar, 1 t vanilla and 1/8 t salt.

Beat till creamy. If too thick add drops of milk. If too thin add powdered sugar a teaspoon at a time.

Dorothy Van Amber
Green Bay, Wisconsin

---

4 Minute Frosting

Combine in double boiler with water in bottom boiling but heat turned off:
2 egg whites
1 c sugar
1/4 t cream of tartar
1/8 t salt
4 T cold water

Beat with beater till spreading consistency.
If desired melt 2 sq. chocolate with 2 T Crisco and pour over frosting.

Mrs. Schubert

Inexpensive Spice Cake

Because there was usually buttermilk and lard available in the home this spice cake was a favorite of most households. Served with either whipped cream or icing it was excellent, but most often this fresh warm spicy cake disappeared before the finishing touches were added.

Mix together 1 c sugar with 1/2 c lard.

Add 1 egg and 1 c buttermilk.

Sift together 2 c flour, 1 t soda, 1/2 t cloves, 1 t cinnamon, 1/8 t salt and 1/8 t nutmeg.

Bake at 350°. Test for doneness with toothpick.

Lazy Daisy Cake

Heat 1/2 c milk with 1 T butter.

Beat 2 eggs until very light .

Add 1 c sugar and beat well.

Add the warm milk and butter and 1 t vanilla alternately with 1 c flour, 1 t baking powder, and 1/2 t salt.

Bake in 8x8" greased and floured pan at 325° for 30 minutes.

While still warm cover with 2/3 c brown sugar mixed with 3 T cream, 2 T melted butter and 1 c coconut. Place under broiler until it begins to bubble.

Lemon Creme Cake

Cream 1/2 c sugar with 1/2 c butter till light.

Add Juice of 1/2 lemon and rind of whole lemon, mix well.

Sift 3 c flour with 1/2 t baking powder.

Add alternately with 1 c water, beating after each addition.

Beat 4 egg whites until stiff but not dry. Fold into batter gently.

Bake at 325° until it springs back when touched or when toothpick comes out clean.

From the McNess cookbook.
Dolly Arneson
Detroit, Michigan

Soft Ginger Bread

Mix 1/2 c butter with 1/2 c sugar.

Beat in 1 c molasses and 1 egg.

Add 3 c flour along with 1 c boiling water to which has been added 1/2 t soda. Stir into dough quickly.

Season with 1/2 t ginger and 1/2 t cinnamon.

Bake at 350° about 30 minutes.

Serve plain, sprinkled with powdered sugar or with whipped cream.

Fluffy White 7 Minute Frosting

Easy to make and very tasty, this icing was used in almost every home. It's virtually fail proof and looks nice on layer or loaf cakes.

Put 1/3 c water, 1 c sugar, a pinch of salt and 1/4 t cream of tartar in a sauce pan. Bring to a boil and cook until the sugar is dissolved.

Meanwhile break an egg white into the beater bowl. Turn it on high and slowly pour syrup over egg white and beat until it's of spreading consistency. Do not under beat.

Flavor with vanilla, lemon extract or whatever compliments the cake.

In place of water in the syrup you can use left over fruit juice which gives it an excellent flavor.

C. Holland
Berlin, Wisconsin

Tea Cakes

Even though we were a very poor farm family in central Mississippi we always had sugar, flour and other necessary baking ingredients. My mother and her mother often made tea cakes, which we ate unfrosted. Grandmother usually used a scalloped cookie cutter, sprinkled a little sugar on top of the cookies before baking them, and served them on a beautiful large cake plate, so I always thought hers were better. It was the same recipe.

1/2 c lard
1 c sugar
1 egg
3 c flour
1/4 t salt
3 t baking powder
1/2 c milk
1 t vanilla, or 1/2 t vanilla & 1/2 t almond flavoring

Cream lard and sugar, add egg and beat well. Add sifted dry ingredients alternately with milk and flavoring mixed. Roll out on floured board, cut with cookie cutters. Bake at 400° for 10-12 minutes.

Doris Dolph
Schofield, Wisconsin

PUDDINGS

Water puddings were popular and easy to prepare. If you couldn't afford to use much milk in cooking, you still could have delicious desserts. It made any plain meal a good one.

In Plentywood, Montana in the early 1930's the ladies invented a Maple Nut Mold recipe that was superb. It follows:

Maple Nut Mold

Mix 1 c brown sugar, 6 tablespoons corn starch, and a little cold water.

Add to 2 c boiling water and cook till clear.

Remove from stove and add 1/2 c nuts, 1 teaspoon vanilla and 1/2 t salt.

Cool and fold into 2 beaten egg whites. Pour into mold pan. Put in cool place to set.

SERVE WITH SAUCE:

To 2 c boiling water add 1/2 c sugar and 1/2 c butter.

Beat 2 egg yolks. Stir in 1/2 c sugar and 1 1/2 tablespoon flour.

Add to water mixture and cook 5 minutes, stirring. Add 1 t vanilla and cool.

Pour over mold to serve.

(Since uncooked egg whites are not recommended today, substitute 1/2 c cool whip for egg whites. Cool in refrigerator.)

Mrs. Leona Jacobsen
Plentywood, Montana

Poor Man's Pudding

Combine 1/3 c brown sugar, 1 c flour, 1 t baking powder, pinch of salt and 1/2 c milk. Spread in a baking pan.

Mix 1 c brown sugar, 2 c hot water, 1 T butter and 1/2 t nutmeg. Pour over batter slowly,

Bake at 350° for 30 minutes. Serve with whipped cream.

Arline Roggenbuck
Shawano, Wisconsin

Tasty Pudding Sauce

Mix 1/2 c sugar, 1 t flour, 1 T butter and 1 egg yolk.

Add 1 c scalded milk and cook until thick.

Beat the egg white until stiff, add flavoring of choice and stir into the sauce.

Serve on bread pudding or left over cake.

FREE ADVICE

Bread pudding was popular in the Depression era because it made a delicious dessert from almost nothing - stale bread.

Roy Gullings testifies his wife went into marriage with one suitcase, one bit of advice and one recipe. The suitcase contained all her needed possessions. The advice was from her mother who said that if you are out all afternoon, set the table first. If your husband gets home before you do, he'll think you have everything under control. The recipe was the following one for Bread Pudding.

Gullings' Bread Pudding

Butter six pieces of toast.

Beat three eggs in a pan, add 1/2 c sugar and beat.

Add 3 c milk, 1 t vanilla, and the toast.

Bake slowly in oven till custard is set, at about 300°.

It's good as is, or serve with maple syrup, whipped cream or ice cream.

"My wife's mother also told her to give her husband a good dessert and he'll forgive you for the rest of the meal. Her mother did a lot of things right and that included sending her daughter off to the unknown of marriage with this one good recipe. She knew that would be enough.

Today I can bring a bit of the good cooking of the Depression days into my life anytime I want. I just make some Bread Pudding using the same old, yellowed recipe card."

Roy Gullings
Wausau, Wisconsin

Another Bread Pudding recipe:

Bread Pudding

2 eggs, slightly beaten
2 1/2 c milk
1/2 c brown sugar
1 t vanilla
1/4 t salt
1 t cinnamon

Stir 5 c of cubed bread into above mixture. Add 1/3 c raisins and dash of nutmeg. Bake at 350° for 50 minutes (knife test). Serve with cream.

1930's Chocolate Pudding

2 T cocoa
1/2 c sugar
2 T cornstarch or flour
2 c milk

Mix and heat to boiling. Cook until thick.

Irene Treu
Wausau, Wisconsin

CORNSTARCH PUDDING DELUXE

"I read about the typical Depression Cornstarch Pudding frequently and without any fondness. Not so in our house! We had plums, berries, grapes and apples, plus wild grapes. As we opened each jar to eat the fruit, the juice was saved in jars in the basement. When enough was saved, honey and cornstarch were added to make the finest pudding ever. Sometimes it was served in hollowed out corn muffins or cupcakes, but usually in bowls. Since the juice mixture was never the same, the flavor changed with each batch. It was always good. If we could get away with it, we'd eat it hot. If it had a lot of apple juice we added cinnamon or mint leaves, otherwise no other flavorings were needed."

Carl Holland

Stale cake can be sliced thin, dried, crumbled and used for toppings on coffee cake, or for a crumb crust. It can give just the right touch to a simple dessert of a peach or pear in a bit of it's own juice in a sherbet glass.

Carl Holland.

It was a rare household that didn't have rice pudding on the menu several times every month year around. It was an inexpensive dessert, was filling and always good. Besides, it was packed with nutrition and made you feel good all over for having enjoyed this delicious finale to an otherwise plain supper.

Watkins vanilla was the flavoring most often used. You knew it was always fresh and a friendly man delivered it to your door. He even gave away a free Watkins Cookbook after you had purchased $25.00 worth of spices. Or you hoped you would receive one as a wedding gift.

Grandma's Rice Pudding

In a double boiler combine 2 qts milk, 1/2 c rice and 3/4 c sugar.

Bring water to a boil and simmer for 45 minutes.

Add vanilla and 1 beaten egg 5 minutes before the pudding is done.

Serve warm or cold.

Frosted Rice Pudding

Combine 1 quart milk in a 2 quart double boiler or heavy pan with 1/2 c rice and 1/2 c raisins.

Cover and cook on low heat for 40 to 50 minutes or until tender, stirring once or twice.

Preheat oven to 375°. Grease a casserole or individual custard cups.

Beat 4 egg yolks with 1/2 c sugar. Add 2 t lemon juice and 1 t vanilla.

Stir into hot rice mixture. Heat through and pour into casserole or cups.

Beat egg whites until fluffy.

Add 1/2 t salt, 1/4 t cream of tartar and 1 T cornstarch to egg whites.

Add 1/4 c sugar gradually and beat until stiff peaks form.

Spoon meringue over top and bake 20 minutes or until nicely browned.

Serve warm or cold.

———————————

Another popular old time pudding version was the Puff Pudding. Some used shortening while others were made using very little added fat. A good recipe follows.

Lemon Puff Pudding

In a mixing bowl beat 4 egg yolks until thick, about 5 minutes or more.

Blend in: 1/3 c lemon juice
                1 t grated lemon peel
                1 T melted butter

Combine: 1 1/2 c sugar
                1/2 c flour
                1/2 t salt

Add to egg yolks with 1 1/2 c milk.

Pour into 1 1/2 qt. baking dish set in a pan of hot water.

Bake at 350° about 50 minutes or until lightly browned. Do not over bake.

Serve hot or cold topped with whipped cream.

––––––––––––––––

Grape Nuts Puff Pudding

Beat 1/2 c butter, 1 c sugar and 2 t grated lemon peel until light and fluffy.

Beat 4 egg yolks until thick.

Stir yolks into butter alternately with 2 c milk, 1/2 c grape nuts, 1/4 c flour, 1/4 c lemon juice.

Beat 4 egg whites till they hold peaks. Fold into batter.

Pour into 2 qt. baking dish placed in pan of hot water.

Bake at 350° for 1 hour and 10 minutes or until pudding begins to pull away from side of dish.

Serve hot or cold with whipped cream.

Escalloped Apples

Peel, dice, and slice enough tart apples to make 1 qt. Add 1 c sugar, 1 c small raisins, 2 T cornstarch, and 1 1/2 t nutmeg. Mix thoroughly. Transfer to a well-buttered shallow baking dish. Pour in 1 c water or use apple juice; cover and bake slowly until the apples are tender, about 35 minutes. Then uncover to brown. Serve warm with meat, or with cream as a dessert.

Addie's Fruit Cake

Easy to do, this old fashioned spicy fruit cake brings back memories of visiting grandmother. It contains a spice combination perfected many years ago. Very simple, but just right, this fruit cake dates back to over 100 years ago in the McLean family of Menomonie, Wisconsin. It is a Christmas tradition and because it seems to improve with aging in the freezer, they use it throughout the year.

Cook: 2 c raisins
              2 c dates
              2 c water
              1 c lard
              2 c sugar
              2 t cinnamon and 2 t cloves
              Cook until soft, about 5 minutes. Cool

Add: 2 t soda in a little hot water
              1 t salt
              1 c each walnuts and whole Brazil nuts
              6 c flour plus approx 1 more c added gently
              to make a nice soft batter.

Makes 6 small loaves. Bake in moderate oven at 350°. *DO NOT OVER BAKE*. Toothpick test in about 50 minutes, in several places.

Mary's Holiday Fruitcake

In mixing bowl combine 3 c pecans or hazel nuts coarsely chopped, 2 c pitted dates or golden raisins coarsely chopped, and 1 c halved maraschino cherries or candied pineapple chopped.

In another bowl combine and stir together 3/4 c flour, 3/4 c sugar, 1/2 t baking powder and 1/2 t salt. Add to nut mixture, stirring until well coated.

Beat 3 eggs until foamy and stir in 1 t vanilla. Add to fruit mixture and mix well.

Line a 9 X 5 loaf pan with wax paper and grease paper. Pour batter into pan and bake at 300° for 1 hour and 45 minutes.

Cool 10 minutes in pan before removing to wire rack.

Mary Klawiter
Chippewa Falls, Wisconsin

Blitz Torte

4 egg yolks, beaten
1/2 c sugar
1/2 c shortening
2/3 c flour
1 t baking powder
4 T milk
1/2 t vanilla

Mix in order given and spread in large greased pan. Bake 30 minutes at 350°.

Test cake if it looks done sooner. The top will puff way up and brown, and when it cools will settle. Serve with whipped cream.

Learn-A Lot Homemakers
Shawano, Wisconsin

Fattigman

Beat 3 eggs well.

Add 3 T sugar and beat until creamy.

Add 3 T condensed milk (thick cream will do).

Add 1 T melted butter, 2 t vanilla , 1/4 t salt.

Add enough flour to roll thin. Cut into squares and fry in hot fat.

Sprinkle with powdered sugar while warm.

MY FAMILY RECOLLECTIONS

Chapter 9

Cars
Were Heaven Sent

THE 8 PASSENGER BUICK

"Our family car broke down irretrievably, and of course Dad went to the nearest dealer to look for a used car. He couldn't afford any of them. Finally the salesman showed him a long 8 passenger curtained Buick which had been turned down many times because it was a gasoline consumer. It ran perfect and was in excellent condition since the previous owner couldn't afford to drive it either.

Being teen age kids, we loved it and couldn't wait to take it out to a village dance at Urbank, Minnesota, one mile away.

We didn't need a drivers license to drive a car and every boy automatically knew how to drive a car, or so they thought. Harsh instructions were given to go only the mile and back. Gas was hard to come by for my parents.

When I got to the village the kids went wild when they saw the big Buick so I gallantly pulled into town. They called it the Hearse and jumped in, all 18 of them, all girls. They wanted to go to Parkers Prairie, the next village, to a dance. My girl friend lived there. I hardly wanted to show up at her house with my heavy passenger load but it gave me the break I needed to get there. I charged each rider 25¢ for a ride there and back. In fact, after putting the required amount of gasoline back into the car I had money left over, even though some of the girls couldn't pay. A few didn't have any money let alone a quarter.

Much as I enjoyed the big old Buick, the size of the car created a problem for me in that I could never see my girl friend alone. So one evening I decided to drive right on through Urbank to get away from the girls without the usual stop. They caught on to this, and the next time they were out there waiting for me. In fact, one even ran out into the road barricading me from going through.

But we had a great time in that old car, singing and laughing over nothing most of the time. Dad never suspected how many miles I went on those evenings, or at least he never said anything because the gas tank was always the same."

Paul Cichy
Minneapolis, Minnesota

We know how much
　　You love that gal
　　　　But use both hands
　　　　　　For driving, pal

Burma Shave

PEOPLE LEARNED TO HELP THEMSELVES

"If you had a problem you put your mind to it, you figured it out. Such was the case with everything, and bald tires too had their day. Tires were constructed of hard thick rubber with deep treads cut in to help propel the car ahead through rough gravel and bumpy roads. They only wore from 5000 to 8000 miles before they were as smooth as glass. Bald tires didn't go anywhere and certainly not out of a muddy rut. Flats happened all the time. You patched them when and where it happened, night or day, cold or rainy, you fixed it before you could go on. Bald tires were just another aggravation you had to deal with since you couldn't buy new tires all the time.

Finally a young entrepreneur came up with a handmade tire retreader made out of hack saw blades. It took state of the art mathematics to come up with the correct equations to get all wishbone treads to come out even on the 16 inch solid rubber tire. The finished product gave another 5000 miles of service to a set. The young man deserved accolades for his ingenuity, but instead suddenly found himself so busy with his tire retreading he never gave a thought or time to patent his ingenious device."

Harold Stahlbusch
Elk Mound, Wisconsin

Car licenses were due the first of the year and you were issued new plates each time. It came at a particularly hard time of the year and all too often you didn't have the funds available when they were due. To keep from being fined you left all the dirt the plates would hold on them, hopefully not to be observed by the powers that be. It was a big worry when the car was needed for church. The rule was not to miss church, even once.

Our mobile society had it's beginning in the hard times of the 30's. People began moving about looking for work, expecting it to be better elsewhere."

CARS WERE HEAVEN SENT

"In the early thirties we felt very fortunate that Henry Ford came along and used his brilliant mind to build a car everyone could learn to drive. And the price wasn't all that bad. For $350 you could buy a brand new Ford car.

Of course you couldn't just climb into it and go. In the Midwest you had to drain the radiator from fall until spring. Freezing would ruin your motor completely. Antifreeze was unheard of so you drained it after each use. Then when you were ready to go again you'd take the hot tea kettle from the stove and fill the radiator. You made sure you had a warm robe in the car to throw over it when you stopped the car

240

even for just a few minutes. It would freeze up easily. In 1936 this chore was eliminated with the advent of denatured alcohol. But again, you had to know what you were doing. If you got stuck in the snow or mud, which happened quite often and you had to rock the car to get it out, the high octave alcohol could quickly burn your car up.

Before the 1939 manifold heater was available you had no heater whatsoever in the car. You wore warm overshoes over your shoes and men wore spats to cover the ankles. Women also wore the high overshoes over shoes which buckled tight for warmth, and added covers of robes and wool quilts.

The early gassy manifold heaters were dangerous, but as soon a gas heater came along which you could install yourself, it seemed worth it to take the chill off.

Everything wasn't rosy yet however because the windshields frosted over and you either had to install a fan to blow on the glass or you'd have to be sure to have clothes pins with you. The hood of the car was split and you could open one side. This is where you used the clothes pins, to keep the drivers side from closing tight so air would get in, blow over the hot manifold and up on the windshield. You never drove very fast so the hood didn't bounce around too much.

And if you wanted to be the neatest guy around and impress that pretty girl you were taking out, you rigged a radio up under the dash board. In spite of the noise of the car and the radio static, it made quite an impression."

H. Stahlbusch
Colfax, Wisconsin

Keep well to the right
> Of the oncoming car
>> Get your close shaves
>>> From the half-pound jar

Burma Shave

EARLY IMPRESSIONS OF A YOUNG BOY

"I was born in March 1921. One of my vivid remembrances was of Dad driving off with the old 1917 Model T Ford. He came home with a brand new model T Ford. Mother was the reader in the family and was more aware of the impending bad times hitting other parts of the country. She really scolded my father for taking this chance on so much money. He had sold some clover seed and the heavy bags of seed had almost been too much for the old 1917 to pull up our long hilly drive way. He felt we needed a better car. But the money was ear marked for the farm payment. Whatever happened, we enjoyed the new car that would start better, and somehow the payment must have eventually been paid. We lived on that farm all our lives and in time it became a family heritage farm.

When the neighbors heard of the new Model T in our possession they all came over to see it. The new one had a one man top. The old 1917 had the two man top which meant it took two people to put it up or down and it had a center post to hold it up straight. The new one didn't have the post in the center. It also had 30 x 32 tires all around. The old one had 30 x 3 on the front wheels. And the new one came with a new head on the engine so it could burn the new high test gasoline, now called premium. It gave the cars a little more power. Roads weren't all shaved down like they are today. You took the hills like God made them and if the put-put engines didn't go up one way you'd turn the car around and try it in reverse. Most often it worked.

We lived five miles from the village and it seemed there were a lot of evening church services. When I was about five years old I can remember the ride home. The Model T went only fifteen miles an hour and the entire road home was a mass of sharp hairpin turns and steep hills. So it took a while to get home. Mother sat in front, sister Rita sat on the left side of me because there was a curtain. Sister Dolores sat on the right side which had no curtain, but she was the oldest and was expected to know better than to lean over. We were each a year and a half apart in age. I was called Pauly by my Father's side of the family and Buddy by my Mother's side. I sat in the middle on the long ride home because I was considered the baby. I always fell asleep almost right away, and to this day have never slept as well. Of course, all three of us were asleep by the time we got home. Dad carried me into the house and poor Rita, although she was actually smaller than I was, had to walk in, while she was still asleep I am sure. Dolores was instructed to take her hand while Mother gathered up the quilts and carried them in.

I can still remember the sound of the car engine and I was in awe of it's extraordinary performance. I observed every detail of that miraculous machine. I was totally infatuated and obsessed by it. I drew pictures on the backs of old calendar sheets of the engine and it's parts and knew what each part did in the motor. I'd draw the car exactly as it was, with every nut and bolt and belt in place. My parents were surprised at my art work and the next year when I went to school told the teacher that I could draw. From then on, standing on chairs and ladders, I was assigned to mural the black boards for Christmas. I enjoyed doing it because I could do it in class and study time. The school board always remarked about the holy scenes at the Christmas programs."

Paul A Cichy
Minneapolis, Minnesota

———————————

Both hands on wheel
    Eyes on road
        That's the skillful
            Driver's code

Burma Shave

———————————

THE FAMILY CAR

"This particular family car was a Model T Ford. The early Model T's had neither a speedometer or gas gauge. When son Ed was old enough to go to dances his father 'stick measured' the gas in the tank which was under the front seat. The next morning he would measure it again. He knew it shouldn't take more than two quarts of gas to get to the dance and home again. But Ed was on to this and he drove more than to the dance and back, so he would 'stick measure' it himself and if it was down three quarts he would add a quart."

P. Cichy
Minneapolis, Minnesota

A guy who drives
    A car wide open
        Is not thinkin'
            He's just hopin'

Burma Shave

FATHER KNOWS BEST

"Our neighbor cousins were also allowed to take the car to the village dance. The dance tickets were 35¢ each so each boy was given thirty five cents plus fifteen cents to the oldest to buy a quart of oil to add to the car engine. Well, with this money in his pocket he bought three glasses of beer, reasoning that his father was always over reacting about that oil business. On the way home the car started knocking and he burned out a rod bearing.

The word got around and so another neighbor, Herby's father, did not give permission for his son to use the car to go to the dance. Cars were hard to come by and maintenance money was exceptionally tight.

Herby, however, loved to dance and to get out to see the pretty girls. They were cute trying to look like movie star Veronica Lake, with hair hanging loose over the right eye or one single ear ring on the left ear. A few even experimented with the permanent waves and had a totally different look. Herby just had to get out and see what was going on.

So Herby waited until his Dad was sound asleep. Then he snuck out to the car, and with the motor barely idling and the lights off, he wheeled the car out of the yard. The dog didn't bark when a family member came or went, but Herby wasn't so sure what the dog would do when the car drove up past midnight. So Herby even took care of that problem by taking the dog in the car with him."

When junior takes
    your ties and car
        It's time to buy
            An extra jar

Burma Shave

The midnight ride
    Of Paul for beer
        Led to a warmer
            Hemisphere

Burma Shave

A young man had to put his head together to be able to take a girl out on a date. "Usually we had very little money if any at all. If I had a quarter in my pocket, I thought I had it made. I could chip in with three others for gas, which was 22¢ a gallon. We usually had 15 ¢ left, which bought a glass or two of 3.2 beer. What more could a young man ask for? And, even better, wedding dances were free. After dancing all night with a pretty girl, the rest of the week went fast just thinking about it.

Ernie Severson
Glenwood City, Wisconsin

No lady likes
　　To dance or dine
　　　　Accompanied by
　　　　　　A porcupine

Burma Shave

––––––––––––––––

With glamour girls
　　You'll never click
　　　　Bewhiskered
　　　　　　Like a Bolshevik

Burma Shave

––––––––––––––––

She eyed his beard
　　And said no dice
　　　　The wedding's off--
　　　　　　I'll *cook* the rice

Burma Shave

––––––––––––––––

Eeny-meeny, miny-mo
  Save your skin
    Your time
      Your dough

          Burma Shave

_____

These signs
  We gladly dedicate
    To men who've had
      No date of late

          Burma Shave

_____

Drinking drivers
  Enhance their chance
    To highball home
      In an ambulance

          Burma Shave

_____

He tried to cross
As fast train neared
Death didn't draft him
He volunteered

Burma Shave

———————————

Keep well to the right
Of the oncoming car
Get your close shaves
From the half-pound jar

Burma Shave

———————————

Don't stick your elbow
Out so far
It might go home
In another car

Burma Shave

———————————

She will flood
>   Your face with kisses
>   Cause you smell
>   So darn delicious

Burma Shave

Doesn't kiss you
>   Like she useter?
>   Perhaps she's seen
>   A smoother rooster

Burma Shave

With a sleek cheek
>   Pressed to hers
>   Jeepers! Creepers!
>   How she purrs

Burma Shave

MY FAMILY RECOLLECTIONS

Chapter 10

They Taught the 3 R's:
Reading
Respect
Responsibility

TEACHERS WERE YOUNG AND RESPONSIBLE

Being a young teacher in a rural school required more than the usual year of normal training to be prepared for the task. The young lady needed a lot of common sense. Fortunately, children grew up fast and were expected to assume adult roles when very young, which prepared the girls well for teaching positions.

The teacher took the place of two parents for 20 or 30 children of all ages for seven hours a day, plus an occasional reprimand session with a spirited one. Each day brought new situations which called for mature judgments. Teachers wanted to do their very best to assure parents their children were in good hands. And they had to make sure that each child was learning and not left behind.

Before this strenuous day began there were the usual details to be dealt with. Not having water in the buildings, teams of students were delegated for each day of the week to carry fresh water from the closest neighbor for the drinking fountain and for washing hands.

Coal from a shed behind the school also required team work to keep the bin full. Because buckets were quite heavy the upper grade boys were assigned to this.

There were chores after class as well, with the floors needing sweeping, chalk boards needing to be cleaned for the next day, and the erasers dusted out in the fresh air. Waste baskets were emptied in a special carton for the next days early morning fire starting in the big furnace. Children were a part of the process, and learned to help maintain instead of destroy. They appreciated their education.

Winter days could become bitterly cold. Now and then when a thermometer dipped particularly low, a kind and loving Dad would get up an hour earlier and build the fire for his daughter. This gesture was overwhelmingly appreciated by any young school teacher when she came in from the cold bundled up to the eyes in wool scarves and mittens. It took a while to warm the icy cold buildings.

Music was provided with a Victrola in some fortunate schools. Students learned to sing along and to carry a tune. Christmas programs were planned by the teacher around talents she observed in the class room. Art work was skillfully chalked on the slate walls in Christmas scenes by the best little artists and some proved to be surprisingly good. Proud parents were amazed and amused at the talented performances at Christmas programs. The teacher invariably knew how to bring out the best in her young charges, hopefully sealing her own future with the school board, especially if it was one of his offspring who brought down the house.

Past schoolhouses
Take it slow
Let the little
Shavers grow
Burma Shave

CHILDREN WERE TAUGHT THE 3 R'S: READING, RESPECT AND RESPONSIBILITY

With thirty some students in a single room, absolute silence was expected and received most of the time. Only when classes were dismissed for recess or lunch break were children permitted to speak freely and visit with each other. Distractions were simply not tolerated. The class in session needed full concentration on the material at hand. Discipline in the school served a dual purpose, with the lower grades often observing what was going on up front.

There was very little fooling around with children either studying their home work or observing the class in session. The point was to keep them busy to use their time well.

If a rule was broken or the teacher disapproved the conduct of a student and therefore sent him to the cloak room or hall for a while, he generally was too embarrassed to let it happen again. Misbehavior was not 'in'.

Staying after school for more serious infractions was also a fact of life. The misdemeanor would have to be written on a tablet hundreds of times to be sure to instill in the young mind that this was one thing you'd never think of doing again. It was when parents got wind of the child's actions that the real punishment came due. There was no getting out of it.

Sisters and brothers told. Children were expected to behave, show respect, and act responsibly with no excuses accepted.

Excerpts from
Hazel Leichsenring
Nebinibuem, Wisconsin

A GIFT OF TEACHING

Isabelle Kelly of Durand, Wisconsin taught school since 1924. Her career began at the age of 19 years, teaching eight grades in a country school. She soon realized she had a decision to make. She loved teaching and wanted to continue with it, but she wouldn't be able to marry and have a family like others her age were doing. You couldn't teach and be married. It was the law.

The young neighbor fellows drove past the school with their teams precisely at recess time to get a glimpse of the beautiful young teacher instructing her classes in games on the play grounds. She hardly noticed them as she went about teaching sport and fairness among her lively students.

Isabelle's career won out and she taught school life long, spending another twenty four years in the Rice Lake, Wisconsin schools.

When teaching in the country, her days began early because it took an hour to warm up the big cold school building.

Insulation was unheard of and the row of tall uncurtained windows all along the south wall to afford sufficient light for the class room was icy cold in winter. Storm windows were not used, it added to the cost and maintenance of the building and was ruled out as not necessary. Most often all eight grades were in the same room.

It was up to the teacher to have the kindling split the day before to not delay in starting the fire in the morning. She had other janitorial duties to do as well after classes before she could gather turned in assignment papers and walk home to her boarding room. It took the entire evening to correct papers from eight classes on each subject and record them all for grading. Isabelle kept close tabs on the children's work, knowing exactly how each student was progressing. If there was a problem, she felt she hadn't done her best.

Discipline was not an issue and parents co-operated with the teacher by demanding absolute respect and obedience from their children in school. If there was a report of misbehavior, the youngster was dealt with quite severely at home. Parents took the time to teach their children to behave and to act like little ladies and gentlemen. The schools couldn't and didn't assume it was their responsibility. Parents expected it from their children and anything less wouldn't have been tolerated. It was considered a family disgrace to have a misbehaving child.

It was not uncommon in the hard 30's for children to come to school without a tablet to write assignments on. They came with pieces of old wall paper or the outdated sheet from the calendar or just anything at all one could write on. Lines were drawn across to make the work look neat and tidy. Mistakes were erased to save the sheet of paper. Frugality was a way of life and any type of waste was frowned on by everyone, everywhere.

Kids left home for the first day of school with instructions from the parents to listen well and do exactly as the teacher instructed them to do. When they got there they found the teacher was firm, demanding silence, and she didn't expect to repeat the rules after telling them once. Even the little fidgeters sat up and took notice of this serious lecture.

The eighth grade class was assigned distribution of the books. Heavy brown paper was handed out with instructions on how to neatly cover the books, gluing the insides of the cover down well with not a drop of glue on the books.

Titles and names were added to the cover with instructions that the books were to be kept in that condition for the entire school year. Of course the covers got shabby and worn but the kids recovered them at home to be sure they wouldn't be in violation of the rules and the teacher would find it necessary to correct them. Books were recycled from year to year and no one wanted to answer to the school board why a book was worn out.

Often the teacher was invited to dinner at the homes of her students. She was popular with the parents and in one family the new baby was even named after her.

When a Mother or the parents had to leave for the day, they often sent the younger children to school with the older ones for the teacher to baby sit them. At times they became a distraction, but as a rule the little ones got so much attention they loved the whole day.

Isabelle Kelly
Durand, Wisconsin

THEY LOVED THE TEACHER

Mary Reiners of Cottage Grove, Minnesota was an attractive young school teacher looking no older than some of her fifteen year old students. In spite of her small size, she had perfect control of her classes.

Boys would get to school early to be sure to be the one to bring in the pail of fresh water for the drinking fountain. Or better still, they wanted to be the first to stoke up the big old clumsy coal and wood furnace. The teacher was always very pleased when she walked into the school room and it was already cozy warm. The privileged boy who earned the chore of maintaining the fire in the furnace had to be very responsible, having learned from his father all about dampers and drafts on the furnace. Chimneys caught fire easily if you didn't know what you were doing. You could never let this happen because fire departments were a long way off.

Mary came to work happy and prepared to do her best. She observed the students closely. If one seemed a bit slow in grasping the lesson she was quick to give him extra attention before the student fell behind. She wanted all of her students to pass their grades with good marks. She worked hard and the children co-operated.

Mary would reward the young students by making recess a fun period. If it wasn't lively games they could all participate in, it probably was drowning gophers again. They did a lot of it since the bounty on gopher tails was a penny for each. Kids had little opportunity to earn money on their own and there were millions of gophers to catch.

Mary fondly remembers the exciting social life of the rural community. There were school picnics where everyone came. The men took time from the fields and came as they were to have a delicious meal with their neighbors. Parents joined in the gunny sack races and the children loved it. Then there were the Christmas programs with the box lunch raffle to complete the evening. The young men were there vying for the teacher's basket, putting a strain on their meager billfolds for a chance to sit next to her. It was a time of fond memories for a young rural school teacher.

Mary Reimers
Cottage Grove, Minnesota

THE SCHOOL PLAYGROUND

"Today's playground is all molded plastic and very fancy. In my time, everything except the merry-go-round was made of heavy metal with a framework of metal and wood. Every school playground had it's tall swing, and we had a jungle gym which hardly resembled today's modern version. Our teeter totter was unique as well, consisting of a board five or six feet long, suspended at either end by chains. It was pumped by the participants on either end to make the board swing freely back and forth.

But the best of all was the 'giant stride'. Chains came down from the top, probably six or eight, and at the end of each chain was a metal hand hold, just wide enough for two little hands. We'd each get hold of a metal bar, then run like crazy around the pole until we got up enough momentum, then lift our feet and take that 'giant stride' until the momentum was lost and we'd drift back to the ground where we'd start all over again running. That was by far our favorite fun thing."

Beulah Tufton
Wolf Point, Montana

At school zones
Heed instructions!
Protect our little
Tax deductions
Burma Shave

THE LETHAL BAT

Edith Allen of Menomonie, Wisconsin was a Tomboy.
Although she was a mere wisp of a little girl, when it came
her turn at bat you had to watch out. The baseball bats were
regular size and Edith was not, and this presented a problem.
Not to be outdone by the big boys in spite of it all, she raised
her bat high and swung with all her strength, hopefully to
get that ball out there just as far as the boys did if not further.

On one such occasion, catastrophe was waiting to happen.
Her little friend was standing too close, and she got the bat
right across her little pug nose and it was broken. When Edith
realized what had happened, she was devastated. Her tears
and crying came so uncontrollably, her bloody little victim
ended up hugging and comforting her friend trying to console
her. Everyone needs a friend like that in tough times.

Edith
Menomonie, Wisconsin

When the stork
Delivers a boy
Our whole darn factory
Jumps for joy

Burma Shave

WORKING HARD AT HOME AND SCHOOL

School days for Buck Stahlbusch of Menomonie, Wisconsin were not to be wasted wishing away the hour. He was busy making the best of it. Sometimes he was generously rewarded with a "meat frying" sandwich for his lunch. It was side pork fried crisp and was about the best sandwich there was. That was because his father raised the hogs especially for the table. The butchering pigs ran at large and they ran themselves lean and were butchered when it was very cold. So there would be lots of fresh pork for the table and lunch pails all winter long. You couldn't eat any better than that.

Buck learned responsibility at school. Most often the water pail assignment was his. It had to be kept filled with fresh water, cold from the pump outside. The waste pail was emptied and washed before leaving after classes each day. And he didn't feel like much of a man if he allowed himself to forget even one time. Prompting from the teacher would have been excruciatingly embarrassing. She was counting on his help. Next week he might be assigned to sweep or to do the blackboards and erasers or carry wood in and ashes out. Whatever assignment any student had, he always wanted to do his best. The teacher expected it.

When you came home there were no end of chores waiting for you. And you were almost never too young to do "exchange work". It took team work to do many of the heavy jobs required to keep things going and neighbors counted on each other.

Women were expected to put a good meal together, especially

when the team work was done at home. Men were proud of a well set table and often wondered how she did it when the pantry and cellar were almost bare in the 30's.

A meal for twenty hungry men could be made out of one old chicken that stopped laying. You simply went out and grabbed the one easiest to get, rung it's neck, dressed it out and the recipe follows. This would also be good fare for a school potluck.

Chicken Pot Pie For A Crowd

Brown in a Dutch oven a year old chicken cut into pieces.

Season with salt and pepper and some sage.

Cover with water and simmer until tender.

Remove pieces to cool and cut into bite size pieces.

To broth, add onions, carrots and potatoes in the amounts needed.

Add more water if necessary to make a large dish.

Add a quart jar of peas or beans along with the chicken pieces.

Thicken the broth with 1/3 cup or more of flour if dish is large.

Pour into baking dish, a roaster will do.

Cover with baking powder biscuits cut with a doughnut cutter.

Bake till nice and brown and bubbly.

Serve with lots of cole slaw to which sweet relish has been added.

Buck Stahlbusch Memories
Menomonie, Wisconsin

WE MADE UP OUR OWN

Children grew up learning to invent their own games and toys. They would come up with some amazing contrivances while at the same time learning to do with scraps.

These childhood experiences were the background of their success when they grew up. No person could go out into the world with a better alma mater.

"I remember we had very few toys to play with. We made up our own. Of course there was no entertainment, not even a radio. It was operated on a car battery, and so to conserve, we were not allowed to use it very often. We made our own fun out of anything that was available to us."

Bea Napieralski
Winona, Minnesota

THE WALK TO SCHOOL

It wasn't easy. Hardships and the long distance to school made a daily burden. If there wasn't anything good to look forward to in the lunch pail, it would be a long day.

A family in Wisconsin with eleven children couldn't keep up with buying shoes for twenty two little feet plus a pair each for themselves. So the siblings devised their own way to make it easier for the barefoot ones to endure the frost on the frozen ground. The ones with shoes led the way, stomping down frost that hurt bare feet, with the shoeless ones following in their tracks. When the season became hopelessly late for the children to come barefoot, a gentle message from the teacher was sent home to the parents.

AARP Mtg.
Menomonie, Wisconsin

NO SHOES

The saddest sound Patricia Trump of Minneapolis, Minnesota remembers hearing in those hard times happened while walking to school in Michigan one morning. She remembers hearing a strange metallic sound behind her, seemingly with every step, and when she turned around she saw a little girl with tin cans tied to her feet with rags.

The teacher had informed the parent that it was much to cold to send the children to school barefoot. The parents had no money and did the best they could.

AUTOGRAPH BOOKS

They have gone by the way of the dinosaur now. We enjoyed the cute little verses in them and reread our books often. Friends would write catchy little verses in each others books as remembrances, generally passed around before school let out for the summer. Two of my favorites were:

> Blest be the tie that binds
> my collar to my shirt;
> For underneath that collar
> lies a half an inch of dirt.

What innocents we were in those days. Or:

> If you get to heaven
> before I do,
> Poke a little hole
> and pull me through.

Beulah Tufton
Wolf Point, Montana

Mom and Pop
  Are feeling gay .
    Baby said
      As plain as day

        Burma Shave

Altho we've sold
  Six million others
    We still can't sell
      Those coughdrop brothers

        Burma Shave

These three prevent
  Most accidents
    Courtesy
      Caution
        Common sense

        Burma Shave

Recipe Index

THE EARTH PROVIDED, Chapter 5

THEIR WORK WAS CUT OUT FOR THEM, Chapter 6

GIVE US THIS DAY OUR DAILY BREAD, Chapter 7

GOODIES OF THE DAY, Chapter 8

THEY TAUGHT THE 3 R'S, Chapter 10